VISIONARY MALE LEADERS

15 Influential Male Leaders on Identifying and Integrating Your *Feminine* and *Masculine* Leadership Traits

EDITED BY SARAH BELLORINI

WM

Visionary Male Leaders

First published in October 2021

WM Publishing

ISBN 978-1-914265-00-6 ebk
ISBN 978-1-914265-01-3 pbk

Edited by Sarah Bellorini & Andrew Priestley

A CIP catalogue record for this book is available from the British Library.

Contents

5 **Sarah Bellorini**
Welcome To The Conversation
9 **Obi Abuchi**
The Strength Of An Authentic
And Vulnerable You
19 **Dimi Cholakov**
Love: The Most Transformational Leadership
Approach In Your Life And Business
29 **Andrew Priestley**
Bad Boss
37 **Simon Hodges**
Leading With Love
47 **Robert Kirby**
Wholehearted Persuasion Skills
59 **Tassos J Stavropoulos**
Leading With Empathy:
How To Become The Leader of Your Life
69 **Phil Bartlett**
The Place You've Always Wanted To Work:
Vulnerability, Trust And Inclusivity
As Business Strategy
79 **Bodhi Aldridge**
Presence

91 **Rick Charlton**
Emotional Intelligence Through Ubuntu

101 **Leon Aarts**
How To Go From Ego
To Compassion And Community!

111 **Jacob Aldridge**
Yes, But How? Six Feminine Energy Systems
Every Enterprise Can Implement

125 **Curtis Harren**
Intuitive Leadership:
Using Feminine Intuition with Purpose

137 **Jaime Galviz**
Tough Love

147 **Dan Isaak**
Visionary Leadership
At A Crucial Time in History

159 **Alan Wick**
Why I Champion Conscious
Empathic Leadership

171 Contribute To Future Editions
Of Visionary Male Leaders

Welcome to the Conversation

Sarah Bellorini

Aggressive. Insensitive. Blaming. Shaming. Toxic.

We all know THIS leader. Maybe we've even been THAT leader?...

Compassionate. Emotionally intelligent. Vulnerable. Whole-hearted. True.

We all know this leader as well.

Which one would you rather be?...

Toxic leadership is ego-driven and fear-based. It's all about '*me*'.

Visionary leadership is birthed from a place of heart-centred desire, integration and authenticity. It is all about what is '*bigger than me*'.

This book is about a new visionary potential within leadership. A visionary leader is one who embodies and utilises inherent feminine and masculine leadership traits – they walk their talk, and their business is not just surviving, it's *thriving*, because of it.

Traditionally, feminine and masculine have been associated with gender however, when associated with leadership throughout this book, they are non gender specific. We are all familiar with the outdated 'toxic masculine' culture – traits displayed by both women and men. Similarly, when we speak of feminine leadership traits, these are embodied in both men and women. By understanding and integrating the feminine and masculine in our leadership approach, leaders are able to rise to and meet the challenges being faced in a rapidly changing culture.

This book is specifically about feminine leadership traits, that are typically over-looked, and the integration of these traits with the masculine. We are all very aware that women continue to be over-looked for C-Suite and Board positions in favour of men however, if the toxic masculine styles of leadership continue to be adopted it won't matter how many women are promoted into these positions – we will simply be perpetuating this destructive culture.

In preparing this title, we've had thought-provoking debates about what *visionary* means... and why *visionary male*? What issues are we acknowledging? The strap-line for our book has been equally debated, applauded, even criticised. Ultimately, this is a discussion about being an integrated human and, it's about integrated leadership.

Globally, top talent is leaving good companies because of bad bosses. Just because someone's job title gives them the status of *boss*, don't automatically assume they are a *leader*.

A visionary leader is someone who can envision, and manifest, innovative ways to impact the world for the greater good. They are not afraid to step into the void of co-creation and hold the space for sustainable change. They have the desire and capacity to impact a future generation of leaders. It is time for us all to change at a fundamental human level.

As Editor it has been a privilege to interact with these 15 authors who have done just that. Reflecting on their human journey has enabled each one of these men to share how their life experience has shaped who they are as a leader in business and, the leadership traits they embody.

Truly global, these men lead significant companies, represent every continent and lead teams from every major culture in the world. Spanning three generations, they offer us unique perspectives that help to contextualize their own leadership lessons throughout impressive careers. Their stories from around the world showcase a wide range of ideas, opinions, insights and practices.

As you read their leadership stories you will see how they have integrated their feminine leadership traits with the more typical masculine leadership style and achieved great success as a result. In each story, we find their experiences distilled into their own personal manifesto of what visionary leadership is, for them.

My intention for you as the reader is to inspire you to think more deeply about your own leadership, and to begin many more intelligent conversations.

Conversations about getting 'comfortable' with the 'uncomfortable'; conversations that begin a much bigger discussion, and; conversations that ultimately start with ourselves, where we learn to integrate our own inherent feminine and masculine leadership traits, and ultimately; in doing so, become visionary leaders.

Sarah Bellorini (Editor)

Sarah Bellorini is an ICF Certified and Accredited Energy Leadership™ Coach, Artist and Author.

She connects professionals on innovative leadership to create change that matters in and through business. Through her unique blend of analytical and artistic methods she helps visionaries align their authentic self + their authentic mission so they can create sustainable change in their lives and the lives of others.

Passionate about people, profit and planet she draws on her 25 years' experience in corporate strategy. She is a member of the International Coaching Federation (ICF), an Energy Leadership™ Master Practitioner (ELI-MP) and holds an MA level qualification in the field of Art Therapy. A beach-loving Australian, she currently lives in the UK with her husband James.

Contact Sarah Bellorini

www.sarahbellorini.com

https://www.linkedin.com/in/sarahbellorini

The Strength Of An Authentic And Vulnerable You

Obi Abuchi

"When we long for life without difficulties, remind us that oaks grow strong in contrary winds and diamonds are made under pressure."
Peter Marshall

Life and business are full of challenges and pain — whether that's navigating changing market conditions or recovering from life-threatening illnesses, addressing resourcing concerns or dealing with a divorce, stemming cash flow problems or handling the uncertainty of being furloughed, driving up engagement and productivity across your business or dealing with the loss of loved ones.

Some challenges are easy to deal with and so you move on, chalking it up to experience. Other challenges, however, rock you to your very core and that's when you begin to discover what you're truly made of as a leader.

In March 2020, when the pandemic resulted in a lockdown here in the UK, and across many parts of the world, all of my business plans and goals were thrown into disarray. Seventy-five percent of my business' income immediately dried up as international travel stalled. On top of that my wife and I had to contend with home-schooling and the various arrangements for all three of our boys, who were in different schools. As tough as all that was, we were aware of the luxury of having good health and fulfilling lives.

However, the challenges didn't stop there!

Our home had a slow water leak that had caused major damage to our property over time. Eventually, it meant that we had to move into temporary accommodation for two weeks in November 2020 while it was getting resolved.

Did I say two weeks? Well, three exhausting months later, we finally moved back home.

I could say that was all that was going on during that time. But, if I did, I'd be lying.

I was also having to face up to a more painful part of my life — supporting my mum who had been diagnosed with Alzheimer's in 2014. At the time of the pandemic, her Alzheimer's was so bad that she'd gone missing several times, including one overnight disappearance that almost sparked a national search by the police. To this day, my sister and I still don't know where our mum was during that night.

Keeping her safe during the pandemic took on a new meaning. She didn't understand what was going on or why she couldn't go out or why she was no longer visiting the day centre. Once again, we had to deal with several instances of her going missing. Eventually, and very sadly, for her own safety, my sister and I had to make the tough decision of moving mum into a care home. Two weeks later, a few days before Christmas 2020, the UK entered another lockdown. Little did we know that it wouldn't be until March 2021 that we'd get to see her again.

The pain of seeing a loved one suffering due to Alzheimer's is really tough. It's like watching a car crash in slow motion as their identity slowly ebbs away. Now, we had to contend with not seeing her for three months and hoping that she was settling in OK, being looked after, cared for and kept safe.

As I reflect on those 12 months, life threw a lot of painful curve balls my way. One of the hardest things for me was connecting with the pain and accepting the challenges of life without letting them overwhelm, derail, or crush me.

Many of the leaders I coach and work with had similar experiences. Not only were they having to deal with unprecedented business challenges, they were also having to deal with many unexpected personal challenges too. However, as is often the case, life still goes on — clients still need great products, services, and solutions; stakeholders still need updates; teams still need vision, encouragement, and inspiration; and businesses still need to be growing and developing.

So, when life is challenging, when life is painful, when life hurts, what do you do?

Now, you could just say, *Man up!, Toughen up!* or *Soldier on!* in these situations. As someone who helps leaders to build up their resilience, if that's all you say, I can assure you that it doesn't work in the long run. In fact, it's more likely to lead to drug or alcohol abuse, domestic abuse, depression, panic attacks, anxiety, or other mental health challenges.

So, what do you do? Run, hide, or numb it? Many do!

However, there's a much better solution: embracing authenticity and vulnerability as a leader. Brené Brown, the author of *The Gifts of Imperfection,* describes vulnerability as *uncertainty, risk, and emotional exposure*. It's that ability to share our lives with others in a way that creates psychological safety and helps build resilience in ourselves as well as others.

From personal experience, as well as my experience of working with leaders from all over the world, here are seven of the best strategies for embracing authenticity and vulnerability. Not only will these help you respond to life's painful curve balls and navigate the turmoil in a healthy way, they will also enable you to become more grounded and increase your capacity to lead with purpose even amidst the storms of life.

1. Ride the Wave

Few people enjoy painful situations and so we're prone to ignore them, numb ourselves to them or deny the pain. I've faced many challenging situations over the years and I've noticed that the more resistant I am to facing a situation, to facing reality, the more I suffer. It's no wonder that in his book, *Belonging,* Bell Hooks said, "We often cause ourselves suffering by wanting only to live in a world of valleys, a world without struggle and difficulty, a world that is flat, plain, consistent."

Life just isn't flat; it has highs and lows. Like the sea, it has waves. I will get nowhere by trying to fight the waves. However, I begin to make progress when I start to ride them. I've learnt that the sooner I can acknowledge that I'm hurting, the sooner I can begin to heal.

2. Stay Connected

As a natural reflector, one of my character weaknesses is that I typically choose to withdraw from others during painful periods. As a leader, it takes wisdom to know who to share your tough burdens with and when it's appropriate to do so. After all, you've still got a job to do and a team to inspire. It's tough to do that when you're feeling low. At the same time, if you don't have an outlet for sharing your struggles then the pressure will only build and become toxic, not only to you but also to those around you. I've learnt that having a strong and trusted network of people living and navigating life with me is critical. In recent years, my close friends have given me a safe space to work through some of the difficult emotions of grief and despair as I support my mum.

3. Shift Perspective

Shifting your perspective when life hurts is one of the toughest things to do and yet not being able to do it means that you're susceptible to being derailed. I know many leaders who have been in *survival mode* and that has only led to a downward spiral. Shifting your perspective is about seeing the bigger picture. One of the most significant areas of growth for me in the last decade has been learning to see that life is so much bigger than me. Meditation, mindfulness, spiritual readings, prayer and journaling have all been powerful approaches that have helped me gain perspective and shift my thinking.

4. Guard Against Helplessness

Many of life's painful, challenging curve balls can lead to discouragement and even depression, especially when you believe that there's very little you can do to change things.

Whilst it's true that my sister and I can't cure my mum's Alzheimer's, we can take steps to help her maintain some quality of life, despite the deterioration in her health. In life, there's always something you can do, however small it may be. Even the little wins help remind us that although there are a lot of things outside of our control, there are also many things that are within our control. Taking action in these areas can make a world of difference to your focus and positive impact as a leader.

5. Serve Others

Many years ago, I undertook a 30-day *giving* challenge and blogged about it. The challenge involved dedicating 30 days to intentionally giving time, encouragement and support to others, including strangers. It was an extremely rewarding experience and reinforced for me the power of humility; not thinking less of myself but thinking of myself less. When all I see is my pain, I lose sight of others; and that becomes a vicious and depressive cycle. A cliché perhaps, and not always easy to do, but finding ways to serve and meet the needs of others helps you get over yourself. It brings more into your life without you even realising it.

6. Dig Deeper

Tough situations have a way of rocking our world. Personally speaking, they also provide a unique opportunity to see areas in my character or mindset that could do with changing or strengthening. It's an opportunity to ask myself, *What kind of personal growth could I experience here that would be most beneficial? What could this teach me about life, myself and others? What am I grateful for?*

Digging deep to answer these questions also helps me become better prepared for the inevitable challenges ahead. In fact, what many leaders fail to recognise is that many of life's challenges are incredible opportunities to grow in mental toughness, resilience and character. When you grow in the valleys you can better scale the mountains ahead.

7. Accept Yourself

As a kid, I loved Superman. In fact, I still think he's incredibly cool. That being said, I know that it doesn't help me to try and be like him — invulnerable and imperceptible to pain — when my world has been rocked. I've learnt to relax into the pain and say things like, *I just took one for the team*; the team of humanity, that is. Self-acceptance is extremely powerful during times of pain. It says *It's OK to hurt. It's human and natural to hurt. It's OK to struggle. I'm doing OK. I will get through this.*

In that process of self-acceptance, I find that I begin to access greater resilience and self-compassion than I ever thought possible. As a leader, when I can do that with myself, I'm able to do that with my team. Kindness to self precedes kindness to others.

Recently, I was working with some leaders in the aviation industry as they sought to rebuild their businesses following the devastation caused by the global pandemic. As we reviewed their recent experiences and anticipated the road ahead, it was clear that the most resilient leaders were those who were adopting at least three or four of these strategies.

So, what is it like for you?

How do you react, or respond, to the challenges and pain that life throws your way? What do you observe about your foundation as a leader? What do the challenges reveal about your resilience levels? What opportunities for growth could they be unearthing for you? Which of these strategies will you choose to start integrating into your life today?

Many leaders want the convenience of growth, transformation, and a positive impact on their people and businesses without the inconvenience of pain. Unfortunately, life just doesn't work that way.

The curve balls of life aren't things we can avoid.

Rather, when we embrace authenticity and vulnerability as leaders, we learn to lead with a greater sense of purpose, impact, and courage and begin to tap into a strength we never knew we had.

References

- Brown. B. (2010). The Gifts of Imperfection. Hazelden Information and Educational Services
- Hooks. B. (2019). Belonging: A Culture of Place. Routledge.

About Obi Abuchi

Obi Abuchi is a transformational speaker and coach with an obsession for helping leaders grow in personal mastery and so maximise their energy, increase their impact, and build their resilience. He is the Founder and CEO of CORE Leaders International, which provides personal mastery and resilience coaching and training to leaders all over the world. He is also the author of *The Magic of Monday* and *Leading from Your Core*.

He's worked with, trained, and coached leaders in corporate giants like Shell, Deutsche Post DHL, and Tesco to improve performance by redefining and shaping how they engage and inspire their people.

He and his wife, Peju, live with their three sons in Surrey, England.

Contact Obi Abuchi

www.coreleaders.co.uk

https://www.facebook.com/CORELeadersInternational

https://www.instagram.com/obiabuchi01

https://www.linkedin.com/in/obiabuchi

https://twitter.com/CORELeadersInt

Love: The Most Transformational Leadership Approach In Your Life And Business

Dimi Cholakov

It is five a.m. I jump out of bed to start another productive day. While I am tying my shoes for my morning run to the beach, I think about how much I have achieved in terms of business, clients, and money in the past year.

On top of that, I have a lovely girlfriend, I am healthy, and I truly love my profession. However, this miserable feeling that resides deep inside me starts to croop up and overwhelm me. I really can not comprehend why I have it. I even feel a bit guilty for feeling this way because I know I have way more than most people could even dream of having.

Yet, I am still not happy. I am still not fulfilled.

The moment I arrive at the beach and soak in the breeze, the sea, and the sand, it dawns on me that the past few years have all been about *achievement, achievement, achievement*. I realise I have forgotten how to experience real joy and fun.

I find myself asking these questions over and over again: *How can I bring back the fun and joy in my life? Where can I find this long-lasting fulfilment that I am looking for? Why do I feel like I am running out of options?*

If you can relate to the above inner dialogue, I promise that something will have shifted inside of you by the end of this reading. You will learn to use self-love as a catalyst for inviting joy, fulfillment, and prosperity into your life.

Embracing The Transformational Power Of Self-Love

I was born in communist Bulgaria in 1987. My first years were like a quest in a giant unknown jungle, trying to find my true self, as my country was finding itself in the newly democratic era.

Influenced by the already established communist mentality, I strived to be someone who people could see as a great example of a strong, honourable, and successful man. Someone who women would recognise as a reliable husband.

I wanted the approval and validation of the collective (parents, friends, bosses, clients) so badly that I started copying their behaviour and following their view of life.

From the outside, it appeared I was doing great: an A student, high achiever, plenty of friends, great physical health.

On the inside, though, I was constantly walking on eggshells, afraid of not meeting the perfect standards. All of this created a tremendous amount of tension and stress in my life. As a result of that, I lost the ability to enjoy it. I was just living and checking boxes. I felt helpless and hopeless because I did not know the problem, or how to get out of it.

I now know that in the quest to fit the collective's perfect standard, I failed to ask for input from the only person who knew who I wanted to be: myself.

Fortunately, after experiencing an excruciating breakup followed by losing almost all my clients and my home base, I was painfully reminded to look for the answers inside. This chain of events put me in the most devastating misery I had ever experienced.

Working day and night to get out of this misery, I realised that my low state of mind was not coming from these immediate events. They were simply a trigger for something deeper and more fundamental. More specifically, my ability to fulfill the basic needs of my Inner Child.[1] I had to learn to give him what he had always needed...

You might be asking yourself, what does self-love have to do with any of it?

Well, all of us are aware of the transformational power of true love.

Unfortunately, our culture, movies, and books have sweetly convinced us that love is limited to loving and being loved by someone else.

1. The childlike usually hidden part of a person's personality that is characterised by playfulness, spontaneity, and creativity usually accompanied by anger, hurt, and fear attributable to childhood experiences. - Definition of Inner Child Merriam-Webster Dictionary *https://www.merriam-webster.com/dictionary/inner%20child* (accessed 8 Sep 2021).

Thus, we are always looking for love from external sources. We are influenced to believe that this is the only choice we have. We are even willing to disregard our own needs and desires to turn into the person who will deserve the love of these people. We become so dependent on their love that we are afraid that we can not survive or thrive without it.

What if love is way bigger and more diverse than we have been made to believe? The ancient Greeks described six different types of love:

- Eros (sexual passion)
- Philia (deep friendship)
- Ludus (playful love)
- Agape (love for everyone)
- Pragma (long standing love)
- Philautia (love of the self)

I discovered that 'Philautia' is the least recognised, and at the same time, the most impactful type of love. It has the power to change our lives and make us feel more fulfilled than ever. I will illustrate the power of it through a fascinating conversation I had that changed my life forever.

This conversation was not with an older man, whose wisdom was so profound that I was a changed man after meeting him. Nor was it a conversation with God or the godly part of me. Instead, this was a conversation with myself. More specifically, with my Inner Child, who was dissatisfied and in pain.

Let's go back to the darkest time of my life, after my breakup.

One desperate night as I sank into my misery further and further, suddenly, something inside of me made me jump out of bed and tell myself this: *What are you doing? You will kill yourself at this rate. It is time you take responsibility. It is time you face this feeling. I believe in you.*

The next morning something had shifted within me. As if something new was born inside of me, as though a spark had been lit. I realised that the only person who could truly lead me out of my misery was me.

I decided to keep this conversation going. So I went for a quiet walk in the park, and this time I had a dialog with my Inner Child.

Dimi: Hey, it is nice to meet you.

Inner child: Hi... (Angrily.) I have been here the whole time. You have not paid any attention to me.

Dimi: I see... I am really sorry that I have not given you the attention I could have... Can we talk?

Inner child: Yes, go on. (Hesitantly.)

Dimi: Thank you, I appreciate it. Well, how are you feeling?

Inner Child: I feel sad and lonely. No one has time to pay attention to what I want and need right now. I feel the constant need to be someone else, achieve something greater, or have more to be loved.

Dimi: Let me clarify. You feel that if you are your true self, others will not love you. Is that right?

Inner Child: Yes, exactly, that's it — Woooo! (Heavy

breathing). I am so tired of this. I do not want to live like this anymore. I want out… (Crying.)

Dimi: I am so sorry that you had to go through all of this. It must have been so hard…

Inner Child: (Crying.) The only thing I need is to feel loved.

Silence…

Dimi: How do you know that you are loved?

Inner Child: I know that I am loved when I can share openly, and someone is truly present and affectionate with me.

Dimi: I am here for you. What else do you want to share?

Inner Child: I want to be OK with who I truly am finally.

Dimi: Who are you?

Inner Child: I am spontaneous… I am creative… I am imperfect… I inspire people to smile and be happy, and sometimes I disappoint them… I create harmony around me, and sometimes I create chaos… Sometimes I am excellent in what I do; sometimes I am not… I live life as if it was a fun game…

Dimi: Wonderful. You are such a free spirit.

Inner Child: Thank you… yes, very.

In this conversation, a huge change took place inside of me. I found the pillar I had been looking for my entire life. The pillar I can always return to: self-love.

I have learnt that self-love means bringing compassion and understanding to my Inner Child, which has helped me reconnect with myself on a level I could never have imagined.

These self-loving conversations opened the gate of miracles in my practice and business as well:

- Increased the number of my clients five times
- Raised my fees five times
- Quadrupled my bottom line

And the best thing about self-love is that once I learned to embrace it fully for myself, I automatically became a more loving and compassionate presence for other people. I literally turned into a true leader for my clients, family, and friends in their quest to embrace their unique selves and unleash their beautiful potential.

Isn't that magic?...

No, it is not. It is pure love!

In what ways can you use self-love to invite joy into your life?

When you find yourself in a tough moment, remember that the only thing your Inner Child needs is a loving conversation. So please bring yourself to a safe place (in a park, on a walk, in the comfort of your own home) and give it a go, talk to him or her. Go in gently with compassion and curiosity. By doing so, a transformation will inevitably follow.

What is your next step in your own journey of self-love?

About Dimi Cholakov, Certified Professional Coach

Dimi Cholakov's mission as a coach is to help leaders and entrepreneurs get their edge back. He is the creator of the *Six-month Life and Career Accelerator* that helps his clients to return to their childlike enthusiasm for life so that they create from a place of fun and joy.

He has dedicated the last 12 years of his life to studying, contemplating, practicing, and coaching in the area of Leadership and Performance. He is an ICF (International Coach Federation) certified coach. He graduated from one of the most renowned coaching academies, iPEC.

He also holds the title Energy Leadership Index Master Practitioner.

He has been coaching one-on-one and in groups people from McKinsey & Company, Centrica, Siemens Gamesa, Microsoft, National Geographic.

Some of the certifications and pieces of training he acquired in addition to iPEC are Belief Clearing, Mindfulness, Anger Management, Vipassana Meditation, Energy Freedom Technique, UPW by Tony Robbins, and ICF Core Competencies.

Contact Dimi Cholakov

cholakov.da@gmail.com

https://www.dimicholakov.com

www.facebook.com/dimi.cholakov/?ref=pages_you_manage

www.instagram.com/dimi_cholakov

www.linkedin.com/in/dimitar-dimi-cholakov-5b576357

Bad Boss

Andrew Priestley

When I started my first business, we had two, then seven and we went up to about 15 full- and part-time employees.

It was a high-pressure, publishing business and we produced a magazine every fortnight on crazy tight deadlines.

I was supervising the team... *and* had to sell advertising, get approvals, send invoices, get artwork, get articles, photos, design, lay out, screen bromides, pre-press... and... and... and... there were a lot of moving parts.

And, I was probably working 12 to 14 hour days, mostly seven days a week.

I took a few hours off on a Sunday but I was always *doing* something or *mentally managing* something. The computer was always on, and I was always working.

Even though I had a team, I was constantly solving problems. I was a very hands-on, operational boss because *no one could do it as good as me, as fast as me or as reliably.*

So you can see, I didn't have a very good opinion of my team. I saw them as a necessary evil.

There was always some reason why *I can't trust or rely on you...* I would be constantly tying up loose ends, buttoning it down and making sure it went to press on time.

As a result, I was frustrated, impatient, rude and I suspect I was NOT a very good boss to work for. (Notice how I'm disowning my bad behaviour.)

You would find me very direct, very short, very sharp bordering on rude and belligerent. Or you would say I was distracted and impatient. In any case, my people were very edgy, tip-toeing around me.

I wouldn't have said I was abusive or a bully — but it's a wonder I wasn't sued by someone on my team under HR laws that are in existence, still.

I know my team didn't like me... but I didn't care. They were *ungrateful, lazy and unreliable*; and I resented paying them.

The truth is I was exhausted all the time; and close to burn out. And eventually, I hated that business.

But I hated who I was even more.

I was arguing with my wife, and ignoring my kids. I wasn't exercising, I wasn't surfing anymore, I wasn't playing music anymore — the joy had really sucked out of life.

One night I had to drive into the city for a client meeting in a nightclub - potentially, a massive contract at the time. My wife thought I was crazy because the meeting was 1am! We argued about the need to conduct business at that time, and after telling her we needed the money, I drove off.

I remember it was a hot, sticky, summer night and I was driving across a bridge when this *awareness* kicked in... *What are you doing???!!! This is absolutely crazy. This is not how you want to live. You have plenty of money... but zero lifestyle. There's nothing nice about this business...*

You know that moment?

So, I turned the car around and I started to head home, and then I thought, *But it's a LOT of money!*

So, I turned the car around *again* and thought, *Yeah... but look at what you've turning into.*

I probably did seven U-turns before I pulled the car over and cut the engine. By now I am sweating, my shirt is dripping wet. I get out of the car and sit on the bonnet staring at the city lights. And then I just wept for about 40 minutes. I was so frustrated and conflicted.

I know I reached a crossroads moment — the intersection of money and values.

I remember thinking, *This is not how I want to be. I don't want to abuse my family. Or my people. I don't want to be in a situation where the people I love... don't even like me. Where I don't like me...*

After an hour I went home.

Shortly after that, I shut that business down.

Over the next few weeks I did an appraisal of my values.

I *talked* about team and would say *people are*

important... but my behaviours were contrary to that. That's why I was ashamed and needed to change.

Be clear, I didn't improve rapidly. It certainly wasn't overnight. It took time for me to turn that around — but I did. I started to pay close attention to how I was showing up. How I was *being.*

Nowadays, people would say that I'm very direct and assertive... although I think they mean in a *good way.*

People say I am sensitive, patient and a good listener. They say that they enjoy working with me.

For example, when I was the Chairman for a UK children's charity we were dealing with a lot of stress and pressure — especially during the onset of the pandemic in 2020-2021 — and I am proud to say it was a harmonious team who operated wonderfully together.

We were very clear about our mission, vision and values – and it was a collaborative effort. I was conscious to provide scope for team-wide contribution and opportunities for my talented team members to solve problems using their own ideas and initiative.

And the feedback was it was a very respectful, professional, positive and healthy working environment. It was worth the time I invested to figure out my approach to leadership and arrive at that point.

I now mentor leaders globally. Leaders running successful companies across a broad range of industries and sectors. My number one tool of choice is *awareness*, especially around how you are being as a leader.

Yes, you've got to be aware of your legal statutory and mandatory obligations, your compliance and governance obligations. We are increasingly being told to create and implement policies that incorporate diversity, gender, equity, inclusiveness, for example. And as a leader that means you need to figure out how your teams are going to operate within those guidelines or constraints.

And also to carefully consider how best to get your teams to shine.

Recently, I was invited to observe a client in action in a normal team management meeting. I discovered that he was certainly not what I would call positive, sensitive, collaborative, inclusive, reassuring...

Have you ever met someone who, when they open their mouth, they make it worse? They get everybody offside? And that is their default position?

From where I sat, he had no awareness of how his behaviour was impacting his team. *They certainly did!*

I felt embarrassed watching himt because he was how I used to be. Like me he had big goals and targets. And his unspoken message was: *You get paid, don't you? Why don't you just do what you're told! Perform!*

That message.

I had spent time digging around his website and came across the company's stated core values.

One of the listed core values was *Respect*.

At one point, it was so ugly, I called a break and then asked my client: *Mate... what are you doing?*

Being a tough boss. I'm giving them direction...

He honestly thought he was being a good leader.

I pointed out that there was no *respect* in any the interactions I'd witnessed. I wondered, if he was like *this* when being observed... *what was he like when he wasn't?*

Visionary leadership doesn't work if you're not aware of how you are *being*; or impacting others. If there's no acuity about what's going on. If you pay lip service to core values and if the walk doesn't match the talk.

Worse, that permeates right through the whole culture. Your business is a reflection of where your head is at. *The fish stinks from the head down* type thing.

Professionals can handle most things. We accept that we have bad days, of course, but we are increasingly less tolerant of a lack of respect or empathy or patience, for example. Good operators increasingly have no bandwidth for bad leaders. Right now, good people are leaving good companies... because of bad bosses... in droves. I think pandemic has really amplified the importance of authentic professional relationships in the workplace, more so.

I mentor leaders to become aware of how you're showing up.

I get paid to mentor others to do what should be

normal, common sense: *treat others how you would like to be treated.*

Many of my corporate clients have done the box-ticking activity on values and principles and inserted the right words into policies and procedures, but it doesn't work if you lack awareness of how you are *actually* being as a leader of people.

Worse, if you ignore your awareness and dumb down or rationalise non-optimum leadership.

My takeaway for leaders is: your awareness works just fine... *if you don't ignore it.*

Manage the obvious starting with the little stuff, such as: *How am I leading in this moment? Right now?*

I was a bad boss because I ignored the obvious.

My awareness.

About Andrew Priestley

Andrew Priestley is an award-winning executive coach who mentors business leaders globally. Qualified in Industrial and Organisational Psychology he is ranked in the top 100 UK Entrepreneur Mentors.

He is a bestselling author, speaker and he guest lectures in leading entrepreneurial teams at Bayes Business School, London.

He loves gardening, music, working out and cooking and lives in Kent, UK.

Contact Andrew Priestley

linkedin.com/in/andrewpriestley

www.andrewpriestley.com

Leading With Love

Simon Hodges

It was my turn next. A swaggering South African boxing champion had gone into the theatre before me. It was week five of SAS selection which meant we had to give a presentation on a military scenario we'd never seen, described in a three-hundred-page folder we didn't have time to read, to an audience of soldiers and selectors we had learned to fear.

I was outrageously unprepared. In fact, I was so caught up in how outrageously unprepared I was for the next hour of my life, that I almost didn't hear the huge thud that came from the theatre behind me. Moments later the doors split open and the South African was carried out unconscious. After gliding through hundreds of kilometres *yomping* the Welsh mountains, apocalyptic weather, and sleep you could count on one hand, he had fainted onstage.

I don't think my 10-year-old self would have expected me to join the army. I was an emotionally sensitive boy who loved to dream, who read greedily and wrote stories, who treasured escaping into different worlds of my making, who created things with my own hands, and who believed that this world is magical and that everything works out just how it is meant to if you just trust in something greater than yourself — quite the romantic and Utopian vision of life, I know!

We don't think of this kind of sensitivity as being synonymous with the army. Far from it. Our bookshops are lined with the shouty machismo and self-denying willpower of former soldiers who claim to have honed the one and only formula for success. We see gilded lapels and rows of medals as a proof of concept. If it worked for them, it must work for us. And, in truth, during my time in the army I met some of the greatest leaders I have ever had the privilege to serve with. People who never asked you to do something they wouldn't do themselves. People who truly cared about those they were leading, who led without a sense of their own image and ego.

But the shouters invariably won out. The camaraderie and sense of purpose I had sought and then found was often undercut by leadership built on fear. Because it is a fear of loss and of losing which courses through the emotional reticence and fear-based machismo that conventional society would like us to believe is the zenith of truly great *leadership*. Winning at any cost, maniacal focus and relentless self-improvement, binary judgement of others, aggression in the face of the unknown, rationalisation over empathy and compassion — these traits, drawn from centuries of martial idealisation in eras when might really was right, have bled into an accepted understanding of what it means to be a leader today.

In the twenty years since I left the army, having retrained as a chartered accountant (a delightfully masochistic decision!), and then started a new career as a wealth transition consultant and life-coach, I've watched how some of the world's *highest performers* don't just operate on a template of fear-based leadership, they unflinchingly believe it is the only way forward.

What's even more obvious to me now — having worked for almost two decades with these leaders — is that I insidiously learned to buy into their template for success. I began to think that the essential beliefs and characteristics of my 10-year-old self were actually weaknesses, that they were my Achilles' heel holding me back from all the success I craved. What I needed to do was shore up these weaknesses and quieten down everything that made me the person I am. I became someone different, someone my 10-year-old self would never have identified with, though my 51-year-old self now feels real empathy and compassion for.

Three years ago I started to work with a Texan entrepreneur and his family. Brought up with nothing, by his mid-twenties he had found his way to the job of a lifetime at NASA. In the early nineties, before the dot-com mania had set its teeth fast into the business world, he left the beginning of the rest of his life behind... he started out on his own with an idea to write the code for what later became one of the largest investment trading platforms in the world today.

His story is like so many of the incredibly successful people I have worked with. They all hit the same way-points. They all have the same heady ambition and delirious commitment to their dreams. They are the sort of leader we have come to admire. They create *success* wherever they go.

Every time I sit down with these leaders, it quickly becomes apparent that they often use the similar methods to get where they are:

1. Control is paramount. They create silos of knowledge, so that no one, not even their closest family and business partners, sees the whole picture as they do. They are the centre of their little universes and 'Divide and Rule' is the guiding principle.

2. They distance themselves emotionally from everyone around them, often based on a very credible belief that no one can be trusted, to protect themselves from ever getting hurt.

3. They are masters of emotional manipulation and rationalisation and bend reality to suit their own needs and beliefs. Control and judgement are powerful 'tools' that they use to get their way.

4. They operate in the shadow of constant paranoia (fear) of what could go wrong and therefore what they could lose at any given moment.

5. More is never enough...no matter how much they have, they have this relentless drive to win and accumulate more.

But what are the consequences of leading like this? Does the external feedback which yells *SUCCESS!* really tell the whole story?

The problem is that many of us are still working in structures where this sort of leadership really does work. The judgement, the desire for control, the egotism and blind self-assurance, all of it breeds success in the world of relentless transactions, self-interested contracts and 'look at me' conferences, where unshakeable conviction can bend the truth to its will. When everyone is fighting for a place on the ladder, we have decided that confidence – too often conflated with the loudest voice in the room – is proof of competence.

So how do these leaders turn out? What of their families? What of their lives away from the image they have created for themselves? What of their 10-year-old selves?

In truth, many of them are isolated, lonely, and afraid of change. The men — it's almost always men — who were able to take risks which most of us could never even contemplate, are completely incapable of taking emotional risks. The thought of having to be vulnerable in front of their children and partners and the associated fear of losing face and respect, results in many of them only seeking out my help when their families are at a breaking point.

Today, my life is all about teaching my clients that there is another, far more powerful way to lead. And so, when all is almost lost, I show them how to get there. Slowly — oh so slowly! — we start to peel back the layers of fear and ego which they have built up around themselves until, over time, this work starts to manifest in a myriad of unexpected ways.

I am not a great believer in 'aha' or 'eureka' moments. They are perfect for dramatic effect and tend to get people's attention, but in my experience are just not relevant and transferable to the vast majority of us. In reality, most changes of perspective come as a result of the cumulative impact of small but consistent shifts in our awareness. It's like slowly turning up the light in your room using the dimmer switch, eventually the light shines so bright that you really can't miss it.

This is what happened with the Texan.

Over the course of a retreat style weekend in the first few months of my work with his family, I brought the family together to discuss its values and purpose, and to identify the risks which could derail a successful transition to the next generation. On the penultimate evening, we were discussing these risks when his adult children began to voice their very real feelings (their voices shaking as they did so) about some of the more challenging family dynamics issues – you could feel the emotional charge in the room. And rather than getting on the defensive as he so often had before, he finally allowed himself to lead with his heart and started by acknowledging the pain his daughter was feeling, how he acknowledged that he had his part to play in this and wanted nothing more than to heal and to express his love for her.

There were a lot of tears in the room that day.

In the space of just a few minutes, he brought vulnerability, love, honesty, humility and humanity back into the room. The shields were dropped, the pretences put aside, and the energy in the room turned on its head. By this bold action, he gave everyone permission to speak their truth without judgment or fear of retribution. To date, this is one of the most powerful examples I have seen of leading with love; when the stakes were so high and the family in such a fragile and precarious state, he was brave enough to dare to choose a new and uncertain path which completely rewrote the family's future.

Nowadays we seem to be caught between ideologies. We know that much of the world is run on the kind of fear-based leadership I mentioned earlier, however, we're also in the process of uncovering a new approach to the way we live together, one in which mutual understanding, the desire for everyone to win, compassion and acceptance have become the blueprint for the way forward — what I call *Leading with Love*.

And before anyone tells you anything to the contrary, Leading with Love is anything but soft and fluffy. In fact, it is one of the hardest things you will ever do. It requires the courage to make the following non-negotiables in your life:

- Demonstrating tough love — holding people (including yourself) accountable to what they said they would do with and following through with the consequences if they don't.
- Recognizing that you only get the best out of any relationship and truly connect when you choose to take a risk by trusting that person and showing up with vulnerability.
- Seeing that people's differences aren't weaknesses, they're essential to a healthy society and the single best way to manage risk in any family or business.
- Staying curious, challenging yourself, your team and never assuming that your way is the only way.
- Seeking and giving feedback openly and honestly, always with the end goal of personal and team development (not seeing this feedback as personal criticism accompanied with blame and shame).

- Speaking your truth even when your voice is shaking and always with a loving intention.

As I reflect on my own journey, the unrelenting turns towards and away from myself, the breakthroughs and losses, the families reconciled and relationships saved, the pulsing dread outside that theatre, I can clearly see the following:

- My emotional sensitivity, which for years I perceived to be my greatest weakness (toughen up, don't show emotion, don't be vulnerable etc...!), is actually my super-power and allows me to perform at a level I previously aspired to but could never reach. Having the ability to read people and intuitively have a sense of who they are, what drives their behaviour, and what's missing in their lives, is like the emotional equivalent of an MRI scanner!
- We are all born with unique gifts which the universe intended us to bring to the fore, but for so many of us, we are out of alignment, wrought on fitting in with society's expectations and 'bullshit rules' and therefore living compromised and watered-down versions of our best lives.

So Why Did The South African Faint?

I imagine he'd say that it was the physical stress, that his body was done, and he simply couldn't go on any further. Perhaps that's true. Perhaps it was simply the last straw.

Only I don't really think that's the case.

What I believe is that he didn't allow his heart to show itself, indeed, I don't think he thought he was allowed to let his heart show itself. He didn't just dread being perceived as weak, he had been led, as we all were, to believe that there was no other way.

To get up on stage with no preparation, with no sense of where you might go or how the people around you might react, is not a question of confidence, it's a question of vulnerability, of surrender to the unfamiliar and leaning into your very worst fears. If you are to truly connect with those in front of you, you have to override your default defence mechanisms.

And if you can't do this, what if you cringe and cower from the risk of letting yourself be seen?

Well, in my experience, the lessons you avoid will always catch up with you. It might not happen for years. You might even get so far as to think you've gotten away with it.

All my clients believe this at first.

But if there's anything I've learnt in the last 50 years, it's that nothing is without consequence, and years of fear-based leadership might not come back to bite you, but it will inevitably hurt those you love the most, and what could be more painful than that?

Leading with love is one of the bravest things you will ever do, and it is the only way forward if we are to move from a place of fear to one of love, where our hopeful, dreaming 10-year-old selves lie.

About Simon Hodges

Simon's passion is helping transform people's lives and bring them back in alignment with who they were born to be. Simon believes that most of us end up living watered down versions of our best life as we are so conditioned to fit in with society and others' expectations of what is 'right' for us and deemed to be a 'successful' life.

Simon experienced first hand, with a nervous break down in 2008, what happens when you live a life that is not authentic to you and doesn't feed your soul. Today Simon has a thriving coaching and consulting practice working with individuals who are looking for more purpose and fulfillment in life as well as with very wealthy and complex families wanting to empower the next generation to find meaning in their wealth and make it a blessing and a force for good.

Contact Simon Hodges

www.simonhodges.com

https://www.facebook.com/simonhodgescoaching

Instagram: @simonhodgescoaching

linkedin.com/in/simon-hodges-592b4119

Wholehearted Persuasion Skills

Robert Kirby

To become effective in a way that transcends the status quo, leaders must master persuasion skills. This article is intended for leaders who value *personal authenticity* and the *evolution* of those they lead over everything else. I promise you will have a deeper but simpler and balanced view of how self-persuasion is the foundation of all great persuaders.

You will learn to persuade through your own *dreams, failures and fears* and then, wholeheartedly inspire your team, colleagues, customers and prospects to do the same.

This always reminds me as to whether a leader's greatness is founded in their (being) or influence skills or in their (doing) or persuasion skills. I believe it's both the feminine aspect of *beingness* (as in your personal brand) and the masculine aspect of doing as in selling both your vision and products to your team and the marketplace.

Over many years of observation and research, I've concluded that all leaders must be effectively trained in both *influence and persuasion* or what I like to affectionately call the paradox of wholehearted *being and doing.*

Great ideas are rarely understood immediately. If they were, they would have already happened. Every change comes with risks and challenges. It's the leaders role to help people overcome their fear, uncertainty and doubt. Then they can voluntarily contribute their energy and resources behind the leader's shared vision.

In this particular article I will focus on *three specific skills* in the *art of persuasion.* Although I love the audacity and boldness of Warren Blair's *one sentence persuasion course,* which concisely focuses on five important doing skills of brilliant persuaders, I've chosen to take a leap of faith and teach you three of the five skills in a more complex fashion.

In other words, how does the subjective authenticity and transparency of the dynamic between the persuader and the persuaded one reflect both the depth and long term success for both parties?

Another way to express this concept is you can't effectively persuade and provide value for those you lead and support unless you have been empowered to embrace and overcome these obstacles in your own life. Closed-hearted or half-hearted leaders need not apply. Great leaders are 100% committed to become wholehearted authentic persuaders.

The Hero's Journey to Wholehearted Freedom

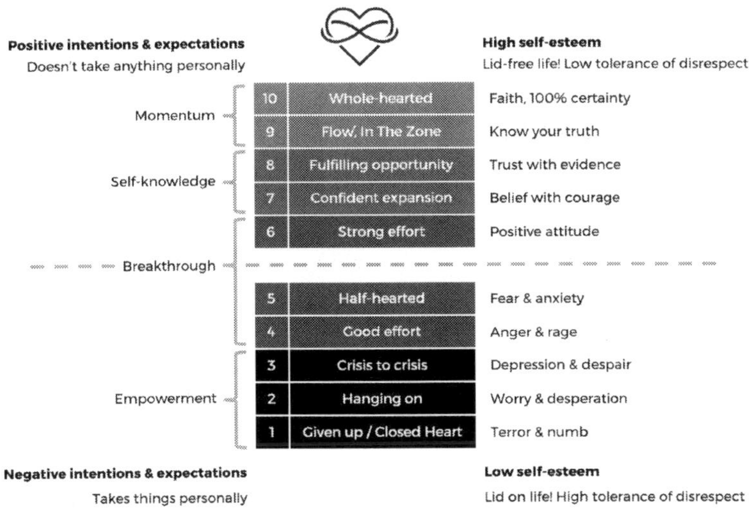

Encourage Their Dreams – By Sorting Out Yours

Everyone has dreams but few people get support for them in such a way that supports their manifestation. Many years ago I was being mentored by a famous scientist – Dr. Valerie Hunt from UCLA. Her background was a physiology professor and researcher of *human energy fields* which took her around the world while she authored many books.

When I met her she was 80 years old. After we completed a six-hour mentoring session in her home in Malibu she asked me to stay another ten minutes to listen to her dreams and give her feedback on her 10-year plan.

I was shocked that someone over the age of 80 had dreams and a 10-year plan. Dr. Hunt lived well into her 90s, wrote more books and gave lectures around the world. Years later I realised she wanted what she called my *boyish enthusiasm for life* behind her. Why?

Everyone has dreams. But they are pre-manifest. They require support and feedback in a very specific way. After they manifest they are measured by statistics, budgets, profit and loss. But when pre-manifest, in the dream state, they require support and feedback. When given wholeheartedly, they provide the dreamer with a pure but powerful intention for their shift from pre-manifest into manifestation. This process changes the dreams from quantum *waves* into a combination of manifesting *waves and particles* unique to creation in the physical universe.

From quantum physicist William Tiller we know intention is the most powerful tool for transformation and creation. Only the thoughts backed up by emotional energy leave the energy system of the person thinking them. They must be positive or dreams remain in the dream state – particles – forever.

Outflow = Inflow is another law of quantum physics which includes the spiritual laws of sowing and reaping or karma. These laws are thousands of years old.

The next step after intention is observation. Your subjective observation of your dream changes the outcome like no other person who ever lived could. It's all about your lens of perception. How clear is your unique and subjective lens?

Moreover, when you have support and feedback for the observation of your dreams, the synchronicity of manifestation kicks in when you have communication with your trusted mentor in place. Thus I emotionally and passionately support leader's dreams wholeheartedly.

Your final step is to create an *authentic attitude* of faith in the unknown with great expectations because then you believe in your dreams wholeheartedly. Attitude effects everything. *You don't want to change one thing but instead everything with your new lens of perception.*

NOTE: Your subjective attitude dramatically effects the teams and customer or client outcomes. You must have all of the above in place *for yourself first* or you all will head down a blind alley. This for leaders is a huge responsibility. Then you can encourage others' dreams with powerful persuasion and magnificent outcomes because they trust your guidance. In others words, it's a wholehearted and authentic co-creation.

Justify Failures – Use Your Life As The Example

Failures are not your fault. You were programmed and conditioned to live and behave in a certain way not only by your family, culture, gender, religion and peers; but also by five generations back on both parents sides of the family.

This is known as the science of multigenerational epigenetics. So the way you live and think, your belief systems and the choices you make are pretty much already in place long before you graduate from high school.

Of course this includes the love, beautiful family support and mutigenerational values that you were given as well as your family disfunction and painful generational patterns that create obstacles and challenges for humanity. So we leaders must take the best and let go of the rest. No mistakes — lessons only!

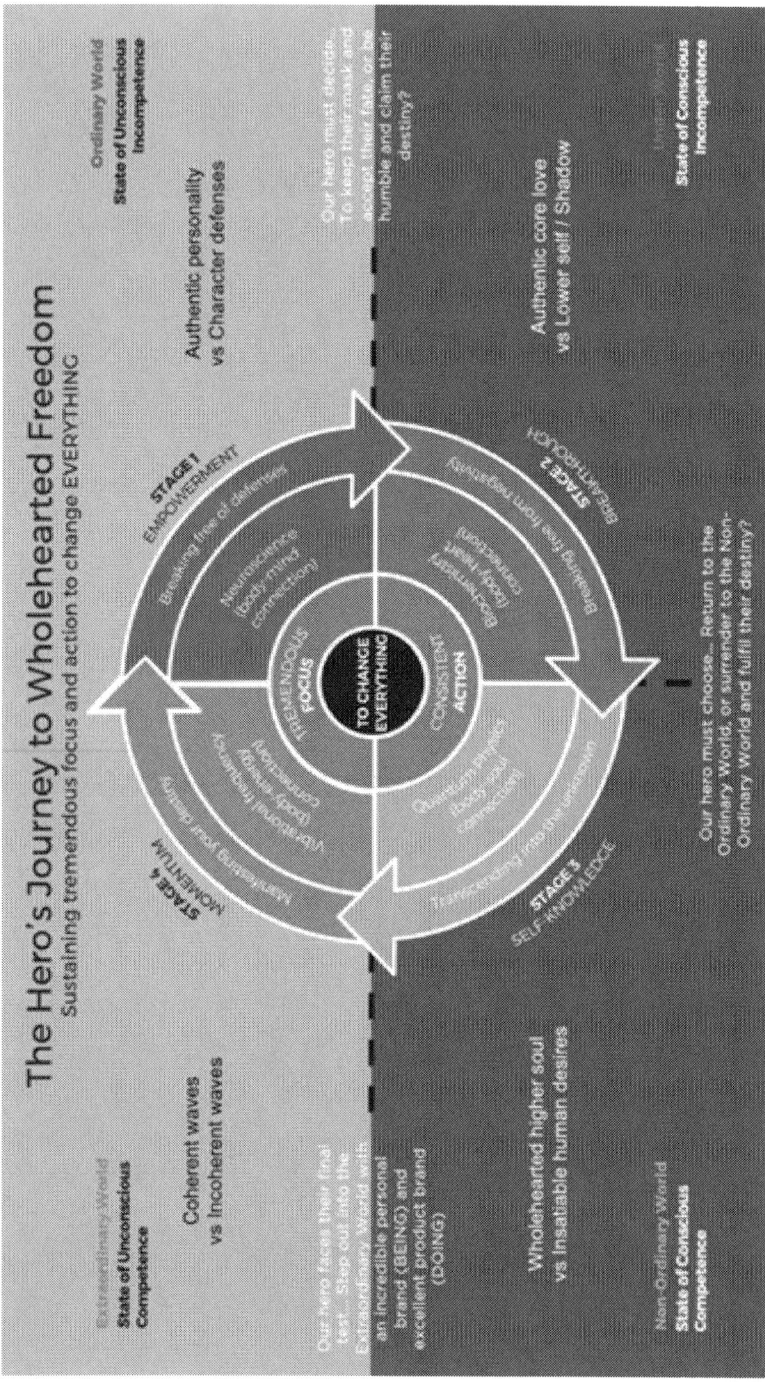
The Hero's Journey to Wholehearted Freedom
Sustaining tremendous focus and action to change EVERYTHING
Ordinary World
State of Unconscious Incompetence
Authentic personality vs Character defenses
Our hero must decide... To keep their mask and accept their fate, or be humble and claim their destiny?
Authentic core love vs Lower self / Shadow
Under World
State of Conscious Incompetence
STAGE 1
EMPOWERMENT
Breaking free of defenses
Neuroscience (body-mind connection)
STAGE 2
BREAKTHROUGH
Breaking free from negativity
TREMENDOUS FOCUS
TO CHANGE EVERYTHING
CONSISTENT ACTION
Quantum physics (body-soul connection)
Transcending into the unknown
STAGE 3
SELF-KNOWLEDGE
Vibrational frequency (body-energy connection)
Manifesting your destiny
STAGE 4
MOMENTUM
Our hero must choose... Return to the Ordinary World, or surrender to the Non-Ordinary World and fulfil their destiny?
Extraordinary World
State of Unconscious Competence
Coherent waves vs Incoherent waves
Our hero faces their final test... Step out into the Extraordinary World with an incredible personal brand (BEING) and excellent product brand (DOING)
Wholehearted higher soul vs Insatiable human desires
Non-Ordinary World
State of Conscious Competence

Your wholehearted hero's journey to freedom must include a process of *letting go* of past programming and *patterns of failure* in order to become free, take your power back and build momentum in business and life.

The first step in doing this is to put the cause of every problem inside yourself. This is the only authentic way to take your power back with your humble heart. Learn to live as the cause of your life circumstances in every situation. Take responsibility for everything and you become the authority that everyone looks up to.

The power paradox: failures are not your fault/ take 100% responsibility for everything.

I learned this valuable lesson between the ages of eight and ten years old. Growing up in Connecticut outside of New York City typically meant that making the Little League baseball team was very important for many American boys.

Baseball was everything to me as a child. I was cut from the little league team at eight years old and again at nine years old. I felt like a total failure and was very jealous of boys both in school and in my neighbourhood who did make the baseball team.

It broke my heart.

I decided to give up on baseball completely. My big brother Jim loved baseball too. He could never play on the team because his asthma was very restricting. So he would not let me give up. He said to me if I did not give up and was willing to practice every day I would make the team at age ten and that the past disappointments – being cut from the two previous seasons does not matter. So I trusted Jim and he trained me every single day.

That summer I practiced all day – everyday.

Well Jim was right, not only did I make the team at age ten, but I was the best pitcher in the league with the most home runs and led the Stratford, Connecticut Indians to the championship. For me that was the whole world at the time. It was the best lesson I could ever have at a very tender age.

That transformation set the stage for my entire life. My brother justified my failures but made me take 100% responsibility to be the best player I could be. Is that not what all great mentors and leaders do? I had to commit with my whole heart.

Reminder, Michael Jordan was cut from his high school basketball team and Steve Jobs was sacked by Apple – the company he founded. Remember what Jordan and Jobs achieved after embracing those setback? They both became the very best – legends in their field.

Accordingly, if you help yourself and others to justify their failures — in other words — the past does not equal the future if you learn and take responsibility for everything — then you can powerfully and effectively persuade them to reach incredible success with yourself as their wholehearted effective mentor.

Allay Your Fears – Then Allay Other's Fears

Fear of life is ranked over *fear of death* in the research on worst fears. Many brilliant leaders are just not comfortable in their own skin. Then when they step out of their comfort zone in taking intelligent risks or often just public speaking opportunities they perceive that they are out of their depth.

My research shows that fears of humiliation (public speaking) and losing what they value most are very common. Often associated with imposter syndrome.

Ask yourself if my fear is rational or irrational? Rational fears include actual health issues, unsafe environments, financial crisis, wars, pandemics and betrayals that have actually occurred. It can be fearfully overwhelming and even traumatising.

Irrational fears such as *fear of life* are complicated. Some fear is really chronic anxiety which means your early wounding is still being projected into the future. It's a symptom of not being wholehearted which blocks both access to courage and self-love. Self-love and fear cannot co-exist.

Is this you?

The most obvious symptom of anxiety is a lack of energy flowing throughout your body – especially the heart including the chest and mid-back.

This means that fear has a hold over you — even successful leaders; CEOs, mentors, coaches, entrepreneurs and speakers often experience this when their business plateaus because they have a lot to answer for.

Your solution is authentic wholehearted flow. It generates the courage to claim your light — your greatness and manifestation capacity instead of contracting into fear and hiding in the bunker.

"Our deepest fear is not that we are inadequate. Our deepest fear is that we are powerful beyond measure. It is our light, not our darkness that most frightens us. We ask ourselves, 'Who am I to be brilliant, gorgeous, talented, fabulous?' Actually, who are you not to be?"
Marianne Williamson

Do you do this? Do you have support to allay your own fears? In other words are you qualified to allay the fears of team members, colleagues, prospects and your customer base? Many brilliant, talented successful leaders will cope with alcohol, junk food, drugs, pharmaceuticals, hook-ups or workaholism in order to deal with fear and anxiety issues.

When you allay your own fears, then allaying the fear of others comes natural. You can effectively guide them to focus on the process and not force the outcome. This becomes your genius as a persuasive wholehearted leader. Great leaders always have mentors and coaches to provide them with support and feedback in order to obtain clarity and effectively allay the fears of others. Great leaders are great followers and that's why they are experts in persuasion.

'The only thing to fear is fear itself.'
Franklin D. Roosevelt

Conclusion

It is so much easier to convince anyone of anything if you as the leader or salesperson are an authentic walking, talking example of what you're promising. So go on then leader, convince me that your dreams, failures and fears are not your roadblock but instead, they have become your launchpad and your inspired catalyst to lead and serve humanity.

This demonstrates that you are the same person on the inside that you are on the outside. You are the leader who inspires people face to face and admires their potential behind the scene too. From this place, your capacity to be an authentic persuasive leader becomes clear and grounded. Your relentless support of those you lead becomes abundantly clear.

References

- Dr. Valorie Hunt - Infinite Mind
- Prof. William Tiller - Science & Human Transformation
- Blair Warren - One Sentence Persuasion Course
- Maryanne Williamson – Poem: Our Deepest Fear

About Robert Kirby

After launching a very successful rise up the corporate ladder in America - Robert decided that facilitating leadership, business development and human evolution skills through a transcendent journey was the pathway to his destiny.

Embarking on this journey over three decades ago Robert has travelled the world and has successfully mentored, trained tens of thousands of corporate leaders, business owners and entrepreneurs. Robert's greatest source of pride and inspiration is mentoring leaders and business owners to become empowered to influence and persuade others to become the greatest version of themselves.

Robert comes with a wealth of knowledge from a life dedicated to mastering the fundamentals of change and growth. His own evolution includes; a Bachelor of Science in Business, Masters Business Administration, Master of Arts in Psychology and Psychosomatics Medicine. In addition, he earned an Advanced Diploma in Body mind-Psychotherapy and Psychosomatics Therapy.

Contact Robert Kirby

robertkirby.com

www.linkedin.com/in/robertkirby-leadership

www.facebook.com/robertkirbyleadershipmentor

robertkirby.swipepages.net/retreat

Leading With Empathy: How To Become The Leader Of Your Life

Tassos J. Stavropoulos

Starting, I would like to salute you for being a person with vision and values; someone that listens with the intent to understand; a smart, sharp, qualified, and influential leader committed to change.

And yet, when you read this article, I promise you will find a way to connect deeper with yourself; become calmer, more settled, grounded and focused. This will allow you to become the leader of your life. It will create the environment for the people around you to be at their natural best; and this will make you a leader in their eyes as well.

Am I a leader? you might ask yourself.

Yes, you are. Even if we don't all have an official leadership role in our work, we all somehow motivate ourselves and others into action; and we do that through the different roles we have in our lives.

The question is not whether or not 'you lead', but rather, 'how do you lead and how do you want to lead'.

So let me tell you a story about how I used to lead and how that helped me to move on, becoming the leader of my life...

During my twenty-year career in multinational companies, I loved to improve effectiveness and efficiency by reorganizing processes and resources. As a manager and a leader, I was action and results-oriented, seeing possibilities and activating myself and others towards the outcome. My focus had always been on getting things done and achieving the results that we wanted with the highest standards of quality. This took a lot of dedication, ownership of commitments, confidence and decisive actions. It also meant genuinely caring for others and leading with authenticity and integrity. On the other hand, my quality-focus and passion for improvement of results, created high expectations towards myself and the people around me in work and life.

It was only a matter of time until the continuous *push* for results would become unsustainable. This happened during an extremely challenging period of my professional career where, due to machine redesign and operational restructuring, people in my team had to work overtime .for a long period of time to keep things running.

Without even realizing I became the *leader* I didn't want to become. My actions were in conflict with my values of respect and genuine care for others. I became a fierce controller and judge and I pushed my team over their limits. I felt a strong energy and need to control and take charge in order to get things done. My *in-your-face* communication was interpreted by others as criticism or anger, even if this was not my intention.

And then my wake-up call happened. I found out *by accident* that one of my direct reports was sharing toxic information against me (without naming me) on social media. At the time I was too absorbed in my *doing mode* to realize that something was wrong. In addition, this was one of my direct reports who, whenever I asked for feedback, was always positive. We had a genuine and authentic relationship together — or at least I thought so at the time. I was shocked. I felt betrayed. I didn't know what to do. I didn't sleep that night. Neither the following. I decided to pretend that I did not know anything about the social media comments, at least for a couple of days, until I would decide my course of action.

The second day, a light-bulb went on in my head. Was my shock justified? How much space did I give to him, when my self-willed *controller Saboteur*[1] wanted to take charge and control of situations and others' actions? How could I possibly know my direct report's real feelings, given that he and his team had taken most of the pressure of the extremely demanding environment we were facing?

In the end, he did the best he could with what he had.

Albert Einstein said: *No problem can be solved from the same level of consciousness that created it.*

I decided to start *being* the leader I wanted, by setting an intention to:

1. Listen more than I talk or give advice.
2. Observe more than I act.
3. Focus my attention on sensing the climate of the 'ecosystem' around me (production team, plant, company).

By putting my attention to listening, with the intent to understand, I felt this was the first time in my life that I truly listened. Most of us, including myself up to that point, "don't listen with the intent to understand, we listen with the intent to reply", as Stephen Covey wisely pointed out.

Truly listening started to broaden my perspective — it felt like the "empathic network"[2] *of my brain was energized. I tapped into the powers of my inner Sage*[1,3]*. I became more empathetic, appreciative and open, day after day.*

As I continued to observe people and sense the climate of the ecosystem around me, I understood that things were not as I previously thought them to be. I realized that 'with the different set of glasses' I used, I saw a different reality. In this reality, the toxic comments on social media were just the tip of the iceberg... I had to take action and I had to do it fast.

And since I could not change the *event* (E), I decided to change my *response* (R) to the event, in order to change the *outcome* (O), following Jack Canfield´s empowering equation for work and life: $E + R = O$[4].

I completely changed the way I communicated with my direct reports during the day. Instead of having formal meetings at specific times of the day in my office, I visited them frequently and briefly during the day at their offices or on the shop-floor. I threw away all the checklists and follow-up tools we had been using during our meetings in the past. The demanding environment and the heaviness of the situation, required the building of trust, together with a sense of lightness, not additional structure, I reckoned. Our meetings became casual and informal, like talking to a friend over a coffee or a beer. I didn't do much of the talking. I mostly listened, I acknowledged their emotions, gave them space and met them where they were.

I shifted from being a controller and judge into being my teams' ally and safety net. I felt our energy shift as well. Then I started communicating more frequently with the first-line employees and the feeling that our energy as a team had shifted was further reinforced.

My negative emotions had almost vanished during the day. Then, when in my personal time at home, I saw a new *toxic post* in the social media, I felt disappointed and frustrated, nonetheless I didn't give up. I knew that everything happened for a reason and this gave me more strength to continue with faith in myself and trust in the process. Our perceptions shape our experiences and our reality.

As Eckhart Tolle said, "If you get the inside right, the outside will fall into place".

After some time, there were no more posts.

Day after day, I felt more and more engaged,

energized, present and connected. I also casually engaged with people from other departments, so as to have a holistic view of the integrated system, rather than just the silo in which I was leading. After some time, I felt the climate of the whole ecosystem had positively changed. Step-by-step we had moved to a new, more human, more empathetic normal. And along with that, came an added bonus: the successful project accomplishment and the efficiency improvement, as a result of our connection that allowed the people to 'be who they are'.

According to the 2021 DDI Global Leadership Forecast, the largest leadership study of its kind, leaders and organizations are undergoing a rapid transformation: they are moving from the priority of driving results to the priority of coaching and developing others, influencing and managing change and developing empathy. In addition, *the number one factor that influences burnout is the leaders´ ability to demonstrate empathy.*

Klaus Schwab, founder of the World Economic Forum, says: "We need leaders who are emotionally intelligent and able to model and champion cooperative working. They will coach, rather than command. They will be driven by empathy, not ego. The digital revolution needs a different, more human kind of leadership".

Empathy is about connection with ourselves and others. It is about listening with the intent to understand, holding space, acknowledging and validating our and others´ feelings.

Off course, we cannot 'make empathy happen'.

However, we can create the space where empathy is present, by being available, open and allowing things to happen. When we allow things to happen, it is easier to let go of expectations, needs and beliefs that do not serve us:

- Let go of our attachments and release the expectations and the thought patterns of our minds.
- Let go of the need to be right and the need to protect ourselves from the judgments of others; accept them as they are.
- Release the need to control and the need to have all the answers.

Shifting from *knowing* mode to *exploring* and *learning* mode, helps us become calmer, more settled and grounded; more connected to ourselves and to the world around us and more focused on the present moment.

Leading with empathy together with using our Sage powers[1] of openness and curiosity, creativity and purpose, pulls us to calm, laser-focused actions. This generates sustainable success and happiness and helps us lead in a more human, humble and yet transformative way.

The above Sage powers, range from feminine empathy to masculine laser-focused action. In the complex and fast-changing world we live in however, everything is interdependent and interconnected, and everything evolves. Labels such as good/bad, right/wrong, masculine/feminine, start to lose their meaning in an evolving world where everything is intertwined.

What is most important, is to lead our lives through positive emotions that 'pull' us into action, rather than through negative emotions that 'push' us and create stress. The latter, in the long-run, does not bring sustainable results and has a negative impact on our levels of satisfaction, fulfillment and mental health. As psychologist and researcher Dr. Barbara Fredrickson suggests, we need to experience positive to negative emotions in a ratio above 3:1 in order to flourish.[5]

Oftentimes however, in our effort to *be the best version of ourselves,* we idealize things, we try hard and get stuck in our tunnel vision, creating expectations that bring us down when not met.

We forget to *be ourselves.*

Empathy gives us a zoom out, more holistic vision. It helps us acknowledge our feelings, embrace who we are with all our fears, limiting beliefs and imperfections.

When we stop fighting ourselves, then we become more open to the world around us. This gives us the courage to address issues that are unpleasant, uncomfortable and difficult for us, because this is the only way to move forward and grow. And then we don't *have to be* the best version of ourselves, because being ourselves 'is' the best version of ourselves.

Leading with empathy is not a not a goal, neither a destination. It is journey of exploration and discovery. Things are not always linear and predictable — you will experience difficulties and negative emotions on the way. This is part of the game of life and part of your evolving process. Even if some things scare you, don't let them stop you. The best moments and the moments of self-discovery, come after struggle and when we stretch ourselves.

Give yourself plenty of space and be kind to yourself on the journey. Do not hurry the journey and do not expect changes overnight.

Be yourself, open and available and you will become more grounded and connected, wealthy with the joy and wisdom you will have gained on the way.

Lead from within and you will become the leader of your life.

Citations/References

- Chamine, S. (2012). *Positive Intelligence: Why Only 20% of Teams and Individuals Achieve Their True Potential and How You Can Achieve Yours*. Greenleaf Book Group Press.
- Boyatzis, R., Smith, M. and Van Oosten, E. (2019). *Helping People Change: Coaching with Compassion for Lifelong Learning and Growth*. Harvard Business Review Press.
- Quach. D (2018). *Calm Clarity: How to Use Science to Rewire Your Brain for Greater Wisdom, Fulfillment and Joy*. Dreamscape Media, LLC
- Canfield. J and Switzer. J (2015). *The Success Principles™ — 10th Anniversary Edition: How to Get From Where You Are to Where You Want to Be*. William Morrow, Harper Collins Publishers.
- Fredrickson. B and Losada. M (2005). *Positive Affect and the Complex Dynamics of Human Flourishing*. American Psychologist 60, 678-686

About Tassos J. Stavropoulos

Tassos J Stavropoulos is an ICF Certified Professional Leadership Coach. He has traveled to more than 25 countries in Europe, Asia and North America, broadening his perspective through connecting with people and exploring different philosophies, societies and cultures. He has a Master of Science degree in Mechanical Engineering and a Masters in Business Administration and for more than two decades was successfully involved in training people, improving processes and leading teams to achieve demonstrable results through various managerial positions in Greek and multinational companies.

The last two years for Tassos, have been a journey of an inside-out evolution, as he rediscovered his compass, listened to his heart and found his true path in life.

True to himself and clear on his purpose, he helps people to follow their passion and embark on their authentic journey to become the leaders of their lives. He currently lives in Greece with his two dogs, Max and Duke, in their house by the sea.

Contact Tassos J. Stavropoulos

stavropt@me.com

www.linkedin.com/in/tassoss

The Place You've Always Wanted To Work: Vulnerability, Trust And Inclusivity As Business Strategy

Phil Bartlett

When you're running a business — particularly if you're part of a larger organisation — you don't have to go far before someone tells you it ultimately all comes down to the cold, hard business results. The numbers don't lie. So as long as they keep going up then you must be doing something right, *right*?

Hire decent people to get the work done, make sure they got paid a decent amount every month, and they'll go home feeling good about working at a decent business.

Caring about your people is a cliché: something for the corporate website or the employee handbook, not for the boardroom. Yeah yeah, of course we want them to do good work, but at the end of the day they're a resource: replaceable if needs be, with loads of people queueing up to take their place if it comes to that. And for them, it's just a job, right?

Let's not overplay things here.

Sustainable Success?

But what if that isn't true anymore (if it ever had been)?

What if we're at an inflection point where our people want more than a paycheck and some free wine at the Christmas party?

In most businesses, particularly in service industries (such as my area of advertising, specialised in health), the quality of the work and thus the future success of the business is intrinsically linked to the quality of the people *in* the business. People are our only real asset and the battle for talent is a pretty unforgiving one.

Okay, so let's put all our efforts into hiring good people, right?

Well yes, but it's not as simple as just hiring good people. You can always hire some good people. Even some great people. But if those people don't feel they can do their very best work, then you're not going anywhere too special.

Or at least, not for very long.

Great people can always do a few bits of great work here and there based on their talent alone, and you can keep that going for a bit longer based on their dedication or ambition. That can even bring you the sheen of success, too, for a time.

But it can't last.

It's not based on anything more than a group of individuals, connected for a short time by their own personal goals and perhaps a personal relationship here and there. When the initial success dies down, there's nothing to keep people from wondering if there's more fulfillment somewhere else.

I know this because I've lived it. I was desperately trying to hold something we'd built together — sometimes through sheer force of character — when really I knew that the castle was built on sand. I could already feel the rumble of ramparts crumbling above me. Drained. Demoralised. Denying the obvious and pushing against the inevitable.

I'm not saying that's how things will go for you, and I wish you every continued success. But there's a lesson to be learnt from the mistake I made:

Success without engagement is not sustainable.

The Times They Are A-Changing

In an ever-changing world, society and community have evolved beyond our recognition. Community spirit (especially in the big cities where our companies tend to congregate) almost sounds like something from times long gone, and the idea of people looking to our political or religious leaders for social cohesion seems even more charmingly archaic.

This is why people's expectations of work have changed, immeasurably and irrevocably.

Alongside a lack of traditional social structure, our people spend more time interacting with each other than they do with their closest family and friends, and they do that in whatever environment we create for them.

So as leaders we have an opportunity — no scrub that: *a responsibility* — to help our people create a sense of community and become the societal glue that we all desperately need as social animals.

The successful people-businesses of the future will be the ones who understand the crucial need to create connected communities for their people: that strive to make every individual feel that they are the missing puzzle piece that makes the sky complete.

Our People As Our Most Important Asset

Take a moment and imagine a place where individuality — in all its many and various forms — is celebrated, embraced and included. Imagine a place where that individuality has space to grow and develop: where the puzzle adapts to fit around the piece, not the other way round.

Surely *that's* how we get towards our great people doing their very best work?

The most important thing you can do as a leader is to get those talented people to feel like they can bring their whole selves to work and express themselves in whatever way works for them.

If you're not doing that, are you just wasting your most important asset?

The uncomfortable truth is that talented people will not put up with feeling that their talents are being wasted. Ultimately, we all have the same needs and if they're not being fulfilled where we are, we will move on.

Over the years I've often found that my background

in behavioural science pulls me into the psychology of how people interact: how we function in an incredibly complex society that we're not designed for in evolutionary terms. I started with an old favourite, Maslow's Hierarchy of Needs and then added how it can be transposed into work-related needs.

Maslow's Hierarchy of Needs* (adapted)

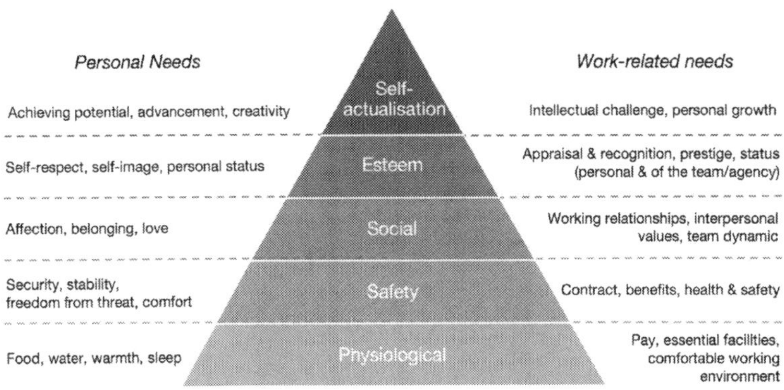

*Maslow, A.H. (1943). "A theory of human motivation". Psychological Review. 50(4): 370–96.

What can we influence in a working environment which can elevate people from the bottom level towards the top, where they stretch themselves, learn more and become the person they always wanted to be: great people doing their best work?

This model was devised as a pyramid because the sections build upwards from the bottom. The physiological needs should be straightforward for most companies (although do be aware not to expect much self-actualisation if the air-con isn't working), so let's have a look at the next one up.

Safety. Sounds easy, right? But our role as employers extends beyond practical and physical safety: we have a huge role to play in emotional safety, too. And that's not so straightforward.

Emotional safety means feeling safe to be honest, or to say what you need in order to do your very best work. It means feeling safe to try something new, to innovate, to create. It also means being vulnerable, feeling safe enough to trust that you can be totally yourself and be accepted, included, and encouraged to succeed regardless of what boxes you do or do not tick.

And just like that, driving an agenda focussed on individuality and inclusivity and safety and care isn't a 'nice to have', it's absolutely central to a successful business strategy as the level of the pyramid that must be solid before people can begin to look up even further.

By celebrating people's differences and idiosyncrasies, and the diversity of thinking they bring to our agency, our organisational design, the services we offer and our creativity, inclusivity (in all its forms) has gone from being an add-on to being a driving force. Great people. Connected by shared values. Doing better work than any of them ever dreamed they could.

And there we have the next thing I've learnt:

Inclusivity is the business strategy.

Your Role As A Leader

The tough part is that you can't just mandate a culture of vulnerability from which all this grows.

It has to start with you.

You have to get your head round understanding that the strongest, bravest thing you can do is to accept your weakness and fear, and share it.

Being able to admit when you're not sure.

Asking for help or support.

Giving something of yourself.

These are not straightforward things to do when you've grown up seeing a version of leadership that doesn't allow you to care too much about people because it might cloud your decision making, or that somehow you'll lose respect.

But you don't have a choice because this is about protecting the future of the business. If you don't aim to create a supportive, safe community, then you can be sure that someone else will.

I know it sounds difficult. Scary, even. But believe me, there's incredible freedom that comes hand in hand with that vulnerability. Allowing yourself to be uncertain. Connecting with your people in an authentic, honest way, full of integrity and care and, yes, love. Still determined, still driven.

And fulfilled like you've never experienced before.

Feelings And Results

What's more, you can begin to take pride in creating a collective where individuality is celebrated and idiosyncrasies are expected. Where inclusivity leads to a diverse workplace in which every single person is uniquely themselves, able to work to the very best of their ability and move up towards being their absolute best self. And that includes you, too.

I know because I've done it.

In truth, I did it wrong first. I hired great people without that culture of inclusivity and authenticity, and whilst it got some good results it wasn't sustainable and left me feeling like I was constantly trying to be something I wasn't. Pretending to be some character that I thought a leader was all about. Occasionally letting someone close to me into the feeling that I didn't know what the hell I was doing. Eventually it completely wore me down.

Then I was given an opportunity to start again, almost from scratch. The brief was to "make this the place you've always wanted to work", and once I'd got my head around what that could mean I set about doing just that alongside some extremely talented and like-minded people. We began with vulnerability and found that it built trust like I'd never experienced before.

Trust connects, inclusivity empowers, individuality thrives. And the collective spirit builds the strongest business you can imagine.

We have since built a place of togetherness, offering solace through a pandemic. A group of people who have remained connected and determined, together. People working with, through and for each other. A place that just feels different.

I had to learn all of this and commit to it whilst running an ongoing business which is part of a massive multinational, reporting to people who report to people who report to Wall Street, every month and every quarter.

Trust me, those folks at the top don't really care about how it *feels*. But they do care about the results that come when great people pull together and deliver amazing work. For us, that's meant our strongest engagement and financial results ever, and a sustained growth spurt during the most difficult business environment in living memory.

Which brings me to the final thing I've learnt.

It's actually all *about how it feels.*

If your people don't *feel* that you genuinely, honestly care, it won't work.

If you don't *feel* like everyone is saying what's on their mind, they're not.

If you're *just not feeling it* (whatever that means to you), you're right.

You don't need a load of data to have a feeling about something. Those feelings come from instincts that nature gave us hundreds of thousands of years ago, allowing us to make judgements without all the information. Ultimately, they're all we really have when we decide to trust someone. Over time, they have helped us build human connections, which in turn created communities, societies and civilisations to fulfil our highest needs at the very top of Maslow's pyramid. Those instincts can help you too, if you can trust them a little more.

Trust that once you have created this environment, you can ask and expect people to engage and commit with clear heads and full hearts. Trust that the end point is good for the business, and really, really good for you.

And above all, trust that the place you've always wanted to work is somewhere a lot of other people would want to work too.

About Phil Bartlett

Phil Bartlett is the President of the CDM office in London (part of Omnicom Group) where he's responsible for ensuring the agency environment is such that great work can be done for local, regional, and global health and wellness clients.

Phil is also the Global Inclusivity and Diversity Lead for CDM and has been a passionate DE&I ally for several years, often called on to talk across the network and industry on gender, inclusion and modern masculinity.

In 2018, Phil was voted as one of the Diversity in Marketing and Advertising 50 male advocates for equality in marketing and media (#DIMA50), before being selected as one of only 30 Agents of Change by Management Today and the Women's Business Council in 2019. In 2020, Phil was included in the inaugural IPA iList as one of 30 trailblazers in inclusivity from across the advertising industry.

When he's not at work he'll likely be found walking in the woods with his wife, their two sons, and the family dog.

Contact Phil Bartlett

pbartlett@cdmlondon.com

https://www.linkedin.com/in/iamphilbartlett

https://twitter.com/iamphilbartlett

https://bartlettbubble.wordpress.com

Presence

Bodhi Aldridge

There is one thing that underpins the evolution of leadership — across business, sport, politics, family and community. And it has become increasingly apparent to me in the 30 years I've spent supporting leaders in these fields and evolving as a leader myself — that one thing is PRESENCE.

Leaders becoming more present. Becoming more connected with themselves. Whether male or female, leadership is an inside-out experience, and so one of the key areas to connect with as leaders is our own masculine and feminine presence.

And so, **what is presence?**

Presence is the internal state of connection with self that radiates our true essence to all around us.

If you have ever been around someone with presence you will experience a calm, grounded, centred person. Someone who can walk into a room and make an impact in a gentle and authentic way — have you ever experienced this?

Presence is where true wisdom lies as it allows us to access all parts of ourselves, our thinking, feeling and intuition.

Presence is a quality that can be cultivated through the practice of more fully connecting with ourselves, cultivating receptivity and flow and allowing ourselves to trust our own inner guidance.

Most people naturally reside more in their masculine or feminine presence. This is not based on gender, yet most men reside in the masculine and most women reside in the feminine.

From this presence there is also a spectrum of qualities that we can draw upon as men or women. There are many, many qualities that could be labelled masculine or feminine or anything else that helps us make sense of the full spectrum of the human experience. And, like everything in life, these qualities can be expressed in an integrated or distorted way!

For the purpose of this chapter, I have defined the following:

- **Feminine qualities** such as empathy, connection, warmth, openness, radiance and magnetism.
- **Masculine qualities** such as independence, agency, focus, direction and purpose, ambition.

All these qualities can be accessed by men and women. A great leader has access to the full spectrum of qualities.

A male leader who has integrated his masculine and feminine qualities in a healthy way can bring more of himself to his leadership.

So, what are some of the essential feminine qualities that a male leader can embrace to bring integration and balance to his leadership?

Over my years of working in this field what I have come to know is that the three most essential qualities are connection, receptivity and flow.

Connection

As we explore what it is to be a male leader, we realise that connection is an essential quality for the masculine.

Whilst the masculine's deepest desire is for freedom, we can only experience this through connection with ourselves. Think about that — freedom does not live outside of you.

As we get to know ourselves, we connect with all the aspects of ourselves: our story, thoughts, emotions, body and being. Our passions, desires, purpose and power. Inner connection is the wondrous exploration of all aspects of the self.

This search is a spiral and can be experienced on many levels in each moment. It is not linear. Learning how to truly inhabit our physical body, developing emotional intelligence, taking charge of our mindset, quietening the inner critic and connecting with our essence and our being will allow us to be integrated present connected leaders.

In my work with leaders, I teach powerful practices to support this connection to presence. Without presence and the ability to be fully present, it is difficult to fully show up as a leader.

This exploration and the quality of connection we experience within ourselves, teaches us to how to create presence and purpose as a leader.

For many a leader, the first challenge is to quieten the inner critic, that busy part of our mind that wants to control or grasp or is always seeking in the external world. Fundamentally driven by fear, it is always looking outward, resisting the opportunity to quieten and become centred.

When we work to quieten the mind, we create space for connection with a deeper sense of ourselves and awaken our creativity, and our abilities to find solutions and to guide our teams and our business.

We also start to fully inhabit our body through connection. We experience the power of our physical bodies and the energy within them. This brings vitality and enhances our presence and the experience for those we lead.

As we experience more of this connection with all aspects of our internal world, our external world changes.

From this place of connection with self, others feel a true sense of connection with us. We create safety and trust in others simply through our connection and our presence.

People feel seen and heard and we can truly see and listen to others.

This is a connected leader.

What does being a connected leader look like to you?

Give yourself a moment to reflect on this... connect with yourself and be open to receive the insights...

Being receptive is the next feminine quality for great leadership.

Receptivity

Until we are open to receive as a leader, nothing truly visionary or innovative can arise. Receptivity connects us with our purpose and the deepest gifts we are here to bring the world.

It is a journey through the heart. It requires openness to all we discover — our joy and pain, our innocence and fear, our desires and our challenges, what we want to create and what we need to let go of in order to create

This is a journey of letting go, of vulnerability, and of forgiveness. To be vulnerable with self and forgive self-first will change your relationship with others.

It takes courage and commitment, gentleness and stillness, contemplation and quietness — becoming truly intimate with oneself.

I recently did some processes in my own life around receptivity and what this has offered me in the leadership space. When I became connected and present, I was able to more deeply connect with my renewed mission and purpose, to feel into where resistance was stopping the flow and open into a space of receptivity.

Within a day came the invitation to write a chapter in this book, within a week came a new client who was wanting exactly what this new mission and purpose were telling me were my next steps.

Out of this I gained space to see and connect with a whole new level of product development and most importantly to deepen and open to another whole level in my relationship with my wife of 40 years. Simply by being present and open to receive.

When we open to receptivity as an essential quality of leadership, we can truly be receptive to our outer world. We can fully open our hearts and minds, put down the armour and defences and fully show up in all our relationships. We feel safe in ourselves.

To be receptive is to be fully available. It is not only about receiving (not *what can I get?*). When we are receptive, we can give in a much more wholehearted way. There is great power in the reciprocity of giving through receiving which raises our energy levels, giving us vitality and a greater presence.

The ability to be open and receptive is essential on our leadership journey, to rewrite the cultural norms through our story. To show leadership from the heart, embracing all that is available to us, both internal and external.

What we then experience in relationship is being open and receptive to all points of view, realising it is about the collective not the individual. Through receptivity we open ourselves to limitless possibilities.

This builds trust and safety for all to show up and be heard and to contribute.

Everybody has a voice of value. Everybody feels respected and accepted.

As a leader you may still have choice and final say, but you are coming from a broader range of creativity, options and possibilities.

This is how we engage and connect the team to a common purpose and vision. This is servant leadership: leading from within. We are receptive and attuned to the whole system.

When we can be fully receptive to a vision created by all, open and receptive and creating a culture based on this, we will incubate incredible innovation, agility, ideas and wisdom.

This is where we truly guide the organisation, receptive to all that is going on, not having to push it and make it happen, rather, supporting it and allowing it to happen.

Which brings us to our next feminine quality…

Flow

Energy is constantly expanding through movement and flow. The feminine essence is constantly in flow as the essential expression of life force.

When we as leaders connect with flow, our lives become more effortless. We are grounded and centred and able to follow the energy of life. We have connected to our deepest self, opened our heart and can allow our truth. We can bring our gifts and purpose to the world.

In sport we see people attempting to create states of flow yet cannot maintain this in their lives. This is because flow comes from the inside. Being connected and receptive in all our lives we can consistently stay in a state of flow.

We are aware that life is energy/vibration, and from this energy we create the whole of our reality.

What vibe am I giving of? Am I resisting in this moment or flowing? Controlling or trusting? Am I present and grounded or seeking and grasping?

In order to create our lives from this energy and flow, we need to take responsibility, internally first, rather than projecting, blaming or being the victim.

Ask yourself these simple questions:

- What is going on for me in this moment?
- What is my inner critic saying?
- How am I feeling, physically and emotionally?
- What do I believe about this situation?

A simple way to check-in whether you are in flow is to notice any resistance. When we resist, we contract our energy and limit the flow.

What does resistance feel like to you: physically, emotionally, energetically and at a thinking level (inner critic).

How will you know if you are in resistance or flow?

Check in with yourself internally. Ask yourself: *How do I resist…*

- my emotions (fear, anger, shame)?
- my intuition (not trusting my gut, talking myself out of things and agreeing with my fear)?

- those behaviours that support me to being present, connected and receptive (sabotaging myself)?

Do I resist external events, not stepping out of my comfort zone, not being willing to receive, not being accepting of other people's opinions?

The healthy response to resistance is always acknowledgement and acceptance. When I fully acknowledge what I am experiencing, then I can truly let go of the resistance and something new can arise.

Resistance comes from fear and often we then attempt to control the external world.

We will manipulate, push, and force the energy to get an outcome. We will defend and be righteous and judgemental. This is a distortion of our masculine qualities.

Trust is the antidote to control. When we work to release control, we can trust ourselves, trust life and stay in the flow. We can trust our intuition as our guidance system and connect to our deepest gifts.

When we trust ourselves, we become leaders who others can trust, allowing rather than controlling, flowing rather than resisting, following the energy of life and our internal guidance system.

Integration

When we can integrate these qualities, to connect more fully with ourselves and those around us, to become more open and receptive, to trust the flow and energy of life within us and all around us, we begin to cultivate a strong sense of presence — we can truly begin to embody a greater capacity for leadership… and this will be evident in the outcomes we create, in the experiences we share, through how we inspire and innovate and grow as a leader.

The leaders I work with are often seeking the next step in their journey. Instead, my challenge to you is to hold.

Before you take that next step, stand present where you currently are: connected, receptive, and in flow.

Can you?

About Bodhi Aldridge

Bodhi works as a mentor and facilitator, supporting leaders and business owners around the world.

He uses a range of skills developed over 35 years as a lawyer and business owner himself, bringing all his life experience to those he works with.

Bodhi has always had a passion for personal and professional development and the ability to combine these to provide clients with maximum impact and outcome.

Knowing that leadership is an inside out job, Bodhi has the ability to gently hold his clients as they explore their inner world to have more impact in their business and as leaders.

Gentle, wise and honest, Bodhi is willing to challenge his clients as he supports them to be the best version of themselves.

Starting out life as lawyer, he then moved into business coaching, training in a range of modalities including systemic facilitation, energy psychotherapy and the art of presence work. Through drawing on such a wide range of skills, Bodhi enables clients to truly connect with their purpose and passion and to experience freedom ,joy and impact, whilst navigating the challenges and ups and downs of professional and personal life.

He is most passionate about the Masculine and Feminine Essence and how the power of these can influence and enhance leadership for both Men and Women.

His personal daily practice includes yoga, surfing, music and meditation.

Bodhi lives with his wife of 40 years by the beach near Byron Bay Australia. They have four children and nine grandchildren which keep them tapping in to the pure joy and innocence that life can offer.

Contact Bohdi Aldridge

bodhi@bodhialdridge.com

https://www.facebook.com/BodhiAldridgeMentoring

https://www.linkedin.com/in/bodhialdridge/

Emotional Intelligence Through Ubuntu

Rick Charlton

'If you want to know the end,
look at the beginning'
African proverb.

Management and leadership are different.

You 'manage' systems, processes, kit and buildings. You 'lead' people. Trying to manage people like a system or a piece of kit will never work. You can't just push a button and make a person do something.

People have feelings, opinions and ideas. What if I could show you a way to create the environment for people to thrive? A way where leaders will also be able to grow, and everyone is happier. A way to achieve:

- increased performance
- higher engagement
- greater creativity therefore more innovation

- lowered sickness absences
- better employee relations.

Ubuntu is that way.

It is an ancient African philosophy. Translated it means *I am because we are.* It's basically an understanding that we as humans are all connected to each other. Ubuntu falls back on one simple concept: that humans were created for togetherness. What drives us apart is greed and lust for power, fancy cars, big houses and designer bags.

I've fallen for it myself (although not the designer bags!). Every time I've chased the money jobs, I've been unhappy. When following my heart, I've been happy. Oh, and the money also seemed to follow by the way.

Ubuntu was the basis of how Nelson Mandela built the new South Africa. When delving further into this it becomes apparent that it is the epitome of emotional intelligence.

I grew up in Botswana in the 1980s.

At that time, Nelson Mandela was still in prison and apartheid was still being enforced in South Africa. Little did I know then the impact he'd have on my life.

Most of my childhood was spent in the bush, connecting with wildlife and living with the local people at home and school. I developed a great appreciation for the African philosophy for life.

At age 13, I had a huge culture shock when I was sent to boarding school in England, I wasn't used to the way things were done in the UK. I did everything I could to avoid school either playing rugby, or with Army Cadets. Belonging to a team has always been important to me.

I joined the British Army at 17 and very quickly ended up in combat in the first Gulf War. Being led through volatility, uncertainty, complexity and ambiguity taught me a lot of things about myself, and the inspirational leader I wanted to be.

I operated all over the world doing all sorts of *interesting things* with leaders from different schools of thought. The inspirational leaders cared about those they led, they always seemed to be there when it mattered in hostile environments. These were men who you would crawl into a minefield for. Then there were those leaders, normally in our peacetime role, who were *process monkeys* who were sticklers for routine and bullshit. Bullies that oozed toxic masculinity. We inevitably had more peacetime than war, therefore the benchmark seemed to be the latter.

One thing I knew was that I wasn't comfortable with adopting this style when I became a leader.

My natural leadership style was very much one of appreciation and understanding. More about getting to know people rather than just telling them what to do all the time. I found that people seemed to warm to me as a leader. I really enjoyed helping people whether it be through mentoring or training.

I was still unfulfilled as a leader in the army. I was struggling. A cog in a machine. Although I didn't know it, I was devoid of Ubuntu. I joined the Fire and Rescue Service because I wanted to help people. I started a rapid ascent through the ranks. I realised people seemed to like the way that I did things. My bosses with the same toxic masculinity I experienced in the army however didn't.

My annual reports were often full of *Rick needs to be more assertive, Needs to stomp his authority on the people who he leads, Must pay more attention to discipline in his team.*

These comments did not sit well with me. I had grown up in a culture, where the main rule was to treat people in the way you wanted to be treated yourself. From then on, I decided to seek out leadership opportunities that would allow me to be myself and role model the power of Ubuntu.

As Head of Change Management in the nuclear industry I endeavour to lead with Ubuntu. I ask my teams working on change management initiatives to:

- Be curious.
- Ask powerful questions that develop a deep understanding of the people impacted.
- Endeavour to achieve true acknowledgement of each other.
- Co-create the change through dialogue.

By truly acknowledging each other we bring each other into existence. In South Africa the greeting *Sawubona* means *I see you,* and the response *Ngikhona* means *I am here.*

That's how engrained Ubuntu is in the culture.

One of the things I have noticed is that there are

many senior women who epitomise toxic masculinity in their leadership style.

These women have fought against prejudice and chauvinism for years. They have sacrificed part of themselves to reach the heights of management or leadership within their companies. This is such a shame because they rarely smile and are openly devoid of compassion for those that they lead. I could see they have so much more to offer. That's how I got into coaching. I helped women and men to reconnect with their feminine attributes as leaders.

It's been so rewarding to see them thrive, to see them happier in their work. Their teams are a lot happier and more productive as well.

When Nelson Mandela created the new South Africa there were lessons drawn out of it based on the concept of Ubuntu. Every day I endeavour to lead with these lessons in mind.

This is the basis of my individual leadership style.

Always search to see a reflection of yourself in others. Look into their eyes and really recognise yourself within them. I find that by simply being truly present when in discussions with others, you recognise the similarities in each other and creates a closer bond.

Always remember that strength lies in unity. There's an African Proverb that recognises this, *A twig on its own will snap easily, a bundle of twigs is unbreakable.*

When leading organisational change, I find that unless you take the time to engage with the people to get them on-board, the change initiative will fail. I've found that team coaching using *Action Learning*

(Reg Revins, David Marquart) develops unity as a team quicker by removing the ego from the sessions. One of the ground rules in *Action Learning* is that statements can only to be made in response to questions, and anyone can ask a question of anyone at any time. This creates a collective strength to enable the change.

Put yourself in the shoes of others. Understand how their life experiences led them to their way of thinking which may be opposed to your own. I've found that by spending time on the operations floor with team members gives greater perspective on their map of the world.

Look at the big picture. Seek to understand before closing your mind to only one option, your own. By choosing to see a wider perspective I find the number of options become greater. This increases your chances of success in any endeavour.

Have dignity and respect for yourself and others. If you respect yourself, you're more likely to respect others and them you. I've found that when I make time to reconnect with nature, follow a good diet and exercise regimen I have a greater level of respect for self. This leads me to respect others also.

Believe there is good in everyone. Strive to boost others' self-belief. I find that when I'm critical of others it is only me that suffers, I don't like that very much. I will never let my opinions of a person be led by others bad mouthing or criticising them, I always make my own mind up based on my experience of that person.

Be hopeful, always strive to hope for a good outcome, and when hope is not as obvious acknowledge it, recalibrate and refocus. I found this important in high pressure emergency or combat situations. If you win the day in your head, you are more likely to win in practice and vice versa!

Reach out and connect with others in conversation. Conversations develop deeper relationships. Some of the most creative and innovative solutions have come from those water cooler chats, or canteen conversations. Always be curious.

Believe in forgiveness. Forgiveness can empower you with self-respect and dignity as hard as it can be at times that's your Ego leading you. I've felt this and have openly reached out as a coach to those who have wished me harm in the past, some lasting friendships have come from it.

Embrace diversity. Draw strength from our differences and turn our backs on judgement.

Find humour in everything you do. As the old saying goes laughter is the best medicine. It also brings us together as humans. I endeavour to never take myself too seriously and ask that my team do the same.

Remember that little things can make a huge difference. I love the proverb *If you think you're too small to make a difference, you've never spent the night with a mosquito*. The smallest of actions can have the greatest of consequences. As a leader, every single contact with people will leave a trace, we must ensure it leaves a positive one, create next level impact. Leave a legacy.

Listen to understand, don't listen to respond. Keep your advice to yourself. I lead with the mantra *advice is my opinion, and my opinion isn't yours*. By understanding and asking the right questions people you lead will think, then learn by application.

My connection to Africa, my love of the people, the bush and wildlife came full circle when I became the Operations Officer for the charity *Veterans for Wildlife*.

On a deployment to Cameroon and leading as an anti-poaching tactical instructor for local rangers in the fight against ivory poaching. I stumbled on some surprising insights.

What made me sit up and pay attention was how the rangers who spoke little or no English responded to my approach, even through an interpreter.

I dedicated the beginning of each session to having a chat with them about their world. Just asking each of them questions to understand their hopes fears and aspirations, also to see how I could help them to be better at what they do. Everyone was given the opportunity to speak. They actively engaged and were open to learn new things. This was down to me taking the time to acknowledge and respect their opinions and wisdom from operating in the bush for years.

On my return to the UK, I reflected upon the culture I was working within the nuclear world. How it was so at odds with the mindset experienced in Cameroon?

This mindset observed in Cameroon was built around leading with dialogue and seeing the interdependencies in everything we do, leading to true collaboration.

So next time you are faced with any leadership challenge, seek opportunities to apply some of these principles of Ubuntu. Observe how people respond to them. What if this simple shift could lead you to a happier, more connected and appreciative workplace?

If you reflect on what you have just read, how has this helped you? I've just told it as it is. I've never looked as deep into my leadership style before. I've always just done it this way.

As we say in Botswana — *Tsamaya sentle* — Go well.

About Rick Charlton

Rick has 30 years' experience in Leadership, Coaching, and Change Management. Currently working in the nuclear industry, he has also worked in the Fire and Rescue Service and the British Army.

Rick is a Director of the World Institute of Action Learning (WIAL), also the Operations Officer for the charity *Veterans for Wildlife* and a tactical training instructor for anti-poaching operations.

Born in the UK he lived with his family in southern Africa from an infant to 17 years old. He embraces every opportunity to return to Africa and contribute by developing leadership capacity whilst immersing himself in the rich culture. He attributes his success as a leader to this immersive approach and is seen as a corporate disruptor.

He describes his work as, *guiding people through leading change in a VUCA (volatile, uncertain, complex and ambiguous) world.*

He also runs his own coaching and wellbeing business.

Contact Rick Charlton

richard.k.charlton@outlook.com

www.ppbresilience.com

https://www.linkedin.com/in/ppbr-2392781aa

Twitter @ppbresilience

How To Go From Ego To Compassion And Community!

Leon Aarts

'I am a single mum, cancer survivor with a three-year-old. I am shielding and can't leave the house. We have been eating ice cream for three days. I don't know what to do. Can you help?'

I received this private message on Facebook in March 2020. It still sends chills down my spine.

The pandemic had recently arrived in the UK and we were a few days into the first lockdown. The streets were deserted and everyone was being told to stay at home. There was a lot of fear and uncertainty around. *How bad is this virus going to be? What can we do?*

The Government hadn't announced what their plan for dealing with this virus would be yet. I could just feel that Londoners would be going hungry.

Immediately I knew what to do.

A simple Facebook post started it all:

Chefs, Foodies, Beautiful People

In these times with so many of us at home I am setting up a kitchen where we, professional chefs, will cook on a daily basis, for everyone who needs it. Whether they're elderly, vulnerable, ill or just need support, we will cook and deliver delicious and nutritious meals to their homes. It's going to be called *Compassion London*. Who can help?'

Within two days I found a kitchen and a few days later we were cooking hundreds of meals, which quickly grew into thousands. There were just six of us in the kitchen on that first day. People started offering their support from all different backgrounds. In those early days we had no website and the food labelling needed to be sorted out.

We all worked hard, *Compassion London* started to come together. Within a week we were cooking sixteen hundred meals per day and growing fast as the pandemic took hold. Our team grew into hundreds of volunteers simply because people wanted to help others in these seemingly desolate and unprecedented times.

The single mother had seen one of our early posts on social media and out of total despair reached out. Our drivers stepped up and committed to driving to the other side of London to give her enough meals every couple of days for her and her daughter.

We were called *Compassion London* because compassion for others is what drove us forward.

The way to start initiatives like this is through having a strong vision and to never waver from your vision. Having the vision and implementing that with courage and commitment comes from our masculine energy. When we connect our vision to our heart, the heart being connected to our feminine energies, the two energies merge. In those instances we have the opportunity to create initiatives which go beyond what we believe is possible.

We step into our authentic power which as a quality is absolutely beautiful. Power is a natural occurrence. Unfortunately, in our modern times power has become force. We have confused that which is forced upon us with power. What we call power in the modern world and society is most of the time masculine power out of balance and not connected to our hearts.

Over time we have totally lost the balance between masculine and feminine energies. We have mostly eliminated the feminine energy causing an imbalance. So much so, that the masculine energy has grown to a point where it has become toxic. It has become toxic because of the lack of natural flow and balance. Feminine and masculine energy act together like a dance, both playing their role equally, supporting each other and taking the lead or supportive role when it's required.

As *Compassion London* grew, I kept communicating my vision clearly; *we will cook and deliver thousands of meals every day*. That's exactly what happened.

My own personal purpose and vision is *no-one to bed hungry*. Throughout my life experiences I have learned how to follow through on this vision with purpose and courage. Because I acted with absolute clarity others felt called to help and could fill the roles which suited them best, organically.

I have always seen my part as ensuring that everyone in the organisation has all the tools they need in order to fulfil their role. Sharing your vision is just the masculine part. To create more beautiful initiatives for the benefit of all it is vital it happens effortlessly. The feminine energy collaborating and flowing in partnership with the masculine energy.

Feminine energy is about community, doing things for the benefits of others, the collective. It is about beauty, colour and creativity. When I think of great authentic feminine energy, I think of a typical mother figure like my own mum or someone else who I know, who really embraces the community spirit, that family energy.

The true feminine energy is about engaging everyone, ensuring everybody is heard, involved and receives their fair share. A mother who looks after a community will ensure that everyone has a meal and will ask questions to ensure everyone feels part of the family.

This is what happened in *Compassion London*.

Once I started the kitchen it was crystal clear what we were going to do. As the leader, it was my focus to ensure my vision engaged the wider community, our volunteers, the drivers, charities we worked with and the businesses who supported us with food and resources. Most of all it was about the recipients of our meals. Each individual is important and adds to the success of the collective.

When you create aligned with your higher purpose, simply for the benefit of everyone, magic will happen and you personally grow too. This is because people see what they can personally contribute, they feel valued and rewarded. When we act from that place of balance, not from toxic masculinity, our energy transfers to everyone involved with creating the space. A feeling of balance attracts others to also come and contribute.

Compassion cooked and distributed 250,000 meals in the first three months.

Wembley Stadium, the home of football, was totally deserted during the first lockdown. Instead of tens of thousands of people cheering the players there were only a few security guards around. The FA Board could see my vision and knew that I had the capability to make it a reality through my work with refugees in the Calais Jungle. They offered Wembley Stadium's kitchens to use for cooking meals and transportation.

I went to see the head of hospitality and the manager of a large global catering company who were responsible for all the food in the stadium. They had shut up shop because of the pandemic and all staff had been furloughed. Initially the catering manager wasn't willing to budge and deemed it impossible for us to use the kitchens.

At the time of the meeting, we were two weeks old and we were still trying to figure things out. Frustrated to see such a great opportunity going to waste I asked what it would take for us to use the kitchen. The requirements which came through were steeped in corporate governance, procedures and due diligence that only a large company could provide. We had none of what they required. I went back to our small kitchen and tried not to let it frustrate me. I decided that I needed to be creative and look for ways to make it work.

I knew we could cook and distribute more than 5,000 meals per day from Wembley.

I went to work and only focussed on the opportunity and how much good we could do. Many in my team told me to leave it, they wanted to stay in our smaller kitchen. I couldn't. I knew that this was a great opportunity to fulfil my vision and all the solutions we were seeking would come to us. Once I committed the solutions came fast. People showed up out of the blue with exactly the right skill sets and experience to help us, from lawyers to food safety experts.

A month after that first meeting, we had all the documentation we needed, and *Compassion London* moved into Wembley Stadium.

In football terms: I always kept my eye on the ball, being the thousands of people, we could feed. It would never have been possible without the help of so many in our community. To me this story perfectly demonstrates the dance between the masculine and feminine energies in order to create extraordinary results.

We brought activity back to the stadium, up to one hundred volunteers per day showing up to help. Drivers collecting and distributing meals. I will never forget the comments of the security guards who said they were so proud helping us and giving their work meaning. The vision and execution came together with the community and purpose. When this happens I compare it to creating a playground for others to come and play in.

I've had my own struggle with masculine energy. Most of my life I thought that I had so much to prove and as a result I never felt good enough. I had taken on the belief that when you're the best in something people will like you and you'll be successful. I developed this belief from the age of eight, just by playing football with my friends.

Early on in my career I became a chef with a very successful restaurant but when someone said that they loved my food or a certain dish I would only hear the voice in my head telling me what was not good enough. I was never satisfied as my driving force was trying to prove myself to others. The tricky thing was that I believed that others wanted me to prove myself and nothing was further from the truth. It was a story which only lived in my head and had become a self-fulfilling prophecy.

It was many years later that I finally managed to let go of this belief. I had a life changing experience at an event in Bali. At the time, I was 41. It had taken me nearly three decades to finally realise I had nothing to prove. Such a simple thing yet it took me many years to realise. I had been living in my head and believed the stories we tell ourselves about how things *should* be, and that success is what's on the outside.

Success comes from within.

On my return home I decided let go of the business I was running in order to become fully myself. To just be Leon. Nothing more. Nothing less. When we go on that journey within (which can be very challenging) we are invited to discover all aspects of ourselves and to harmonise or balance our feminine and masculine energies.

My life changing experience in Bali was 14 years ago and it has been a journey with ups and downs. However, going on that exploration, letting go and embracing all parts of your self is the most rewarding thing you can ever do in your life. You'll discover your own true natural power and how that guides everything you do. The only thing we need to do really is to just get out of our own way.

The story is often told that an acorn knows that it has everything within itself to be a mighty oak tree. I agree with that. When I look at trees I often see them as an example for us. A tree stands there, beautifully still, fully in balance and by doing that everything just happens. There is a whole ecosystem depending on the tree. Birds nest in its branches, it grows acorns or fruit and the tree let's children can play in its shade. It's perfect as it is.

To me, that is the balance of the energies dancing together. A tree just allows the whole ecosystem to collaborate. That is what I believe we humans can achieve in our own way too. Allowing the energies to flow through us creates amazing results, which benefits everyone.

Nature doesn't grow a wforest. It grows trees, plants, birds and insects. A refined ecosystem which depends on each other. All parts communicate with each other and collaborate for the greater good. Nature creates communities. Communities choose compassion and when we do so every part of the community will flourish.

Choose Compassion!

About Leon Aarts

Leon sees himself as a modern day alchemist and philanthropist.

His career spans from being a top chef, to social entrepreneur, a TedX speaker, the author of four books and the founder of three charities. He lives his life aligned with his purpose; no-one to bed hungry.

Currently Leon is Head of Felix's Kitchen. A kitchen built to cook 1.5M meals per year for children, families, and people in food insecurity in London, using surplus food.

In his spare time he cycles, reads, spends time in nature and with his two children. He mentors people to live a more meaningful life, leading by example. A life-changing experience led him to give up his business life and to focus on empowering others.

Contact Leon Aarts

leon@leon-aarts.com

www.leon-aarts.com

www.facebook.com/leonaarts

www.instagram.com/leonaarts1

https://www.linkedin.com/in/leonaarts1/

Yes, But How? Six Feminine Energy Systems Every Enterprise Can Implement

Jacob Aldridge

Let me tell you about Jennifer.

Jennifer isn't real. Jennifer is an average, an amalgam of modern managers, named because *Jennifer* was the most popular girls name for every year of the 1970s, which is when she was born[1, 2, 3].

If (when she was born) Jennifer had looked around the maternity ward, she may have noticed there were slightly more boys than girls. For some reason humans average about 106 boys for every 100 girls born.

But by the time Jennifer graduated from High School that advantage had flipped. More girls graduate from high school than boys. And if she'd looked around her university course she may have been surprised to see almost 50% more women than men graduating with a Bachelor's Degree. That's half as many again, 150 women for every 100 men.

This is the wave of women who enter the workforce. Qualified. Competent. Motivated. Ready.

Then something happens.

Because Jennifer is actually 10% less likely to be employed. Women are half as likely to be employed full-time, and if Jennifer is employed full-time then on average she'll be earning 14% less money... 21% less if she works in a private organisation of more than 100 staff.

She is twice as likely to be underemployed, and has accumulated 42% less for her retirement. Remembering, of course, that more boys are born but women live much longer into old age.

- Women are 37% of the full-time workforce.
- They are 30% of Key Management.
- They are 26% of Company Directors.
- Just 17% of CEOs
- and only 14% of Board Chairs.

One in three Boards in Australia have no women. Only one in 100 have no men. But why?

Well we can point to the recalcitrant misogynists. We can point to the genetic realities of pregnancy and childbirth. But I believe at a fundamental level it's not some individuals or a biological clock that has failed Jennifer — it's the nature of business itself.

Business - as we contextualise it, as we teach it, as you learn in an MBA or from your favourite podcast — fails women because it was neither designed by women nor for the Feminine energy that is most often found in women.

I Am Not A Visionary Male Leader

Modern business has been created by the masculine energy for the benefit of the Masculine energy, ignorant of the power and potential or even the existence of a different, feminine way of doing business.

And there is your opportunity as a visionary male leader. When you embrace the feminine way of doing business as well as the masculine, then you become an employer of choice who leads a more powerful and effective organisation.

For my first successful decade in business, this insight escaped me. I led teams, I coached others to lead teams, and all around the world I did so without ever realising how my business reflected only my natural masculine traits.

I regularly hosted a workshop on vision and strategy in business, a great lead-generation activity that was almost exclusively well-received. And then one day an attendee said that it did not resonate with her at all.

And I thought, "Well, that's just her." Until I realised — she was the first woman who had come to my workshop in months. And when I looked around my team and my clients, even the leaders within my clients, there were very few other women to compare her with. Maybe it wasn't her? Maybe it was me?

We are all a combination of masculine and feminine energy — this is neither binary, nor a gender discussion.

Most of us have a strong tendency for seeing the world and making decisions through one style, and this predisposition does break a little along gender lines.

So nobody would have been surprised that I embodied the masculine energy and masculine approach to business: being linear, analytical, outcome-focused, and seeking growth through future challenges I had created for myself.

Some male leaders are more in tune with, or even naturally revert to, their feminine elements: around connection, relationships, accepting ambiguity, and finding growth from support and praise in the present.

Neither energy is better or worse, even in business. Both can be healthy, or show up in toxic forms.

Strategic planning often reveals the distinction, however. My masculine style aligned nicely with discussions about goals and future states, KPIs, and target measurements that were very linear in their direction.

The feminine normally disconnects from that debate, valuing much more how they feel, and the relationships and values they intend to build and embody beginning with right now.

Have you ever left a strategy day feeling it was all talk, and no action? All future and no present? All masculine… and no feminine?

Turns out the missing pieces that leave Jennifer disconnected, contributing less, or dropping out entirely, are also the pieces you need to fully execute your most powerful ideas.

So rather than ponder the enormous volume of feminine talent that has been lost to enterprise through this outdated approach, let us embrace the opportunity this creates. Because it means business systems that embrace the feminine are not radical or revolutionary — rather, they probably resemble ideas you've had before but weren't sure how, or why, to implement them until now.

The Employee Empowerment Journey

Practical leadership can't see everything as a seesaw, jumping from masculine at one end to feminine at the other and hoping to create balance. This approach is *EITHER/OR*, and leads to exhausted leaders and confused team members.

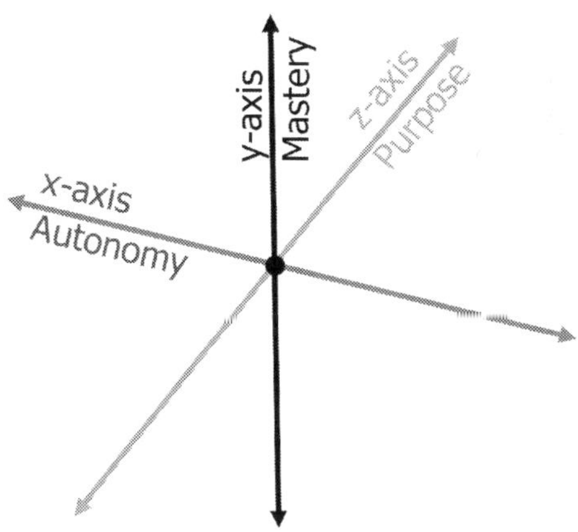

The Three Dimensions of the Employee Empowerment Model

Organisations that build on consistent leadership have an *AND* approach, implementing systems to support the different needs of all their team members. Building on the work of Carl Jung, Dan Pink, Tony Robbins, and others, I embrace the complexity of the humans I work with (including their combined masculine and feminine energies) with the above Employee Empowerment Model.

If you've ever felt that managing people was an endless game of 3-Dimensional Chess, you were right! Every member of your team has the same fundamental human drives, but these motivations are self-contradictory and their importance changes over time.

Only by embracing the masculine and the feminine in our leadership style can we continuously ensure we are achieving all of the outcomes, meeting the needs of a team member who may arrive at work today with different requirements to yesterday.

Dan Pink's research demonstrated that, after money, individuals are motivated by a combination of autonomy, mastery, and purpose[4]. This doesn't mean money doesn't matter – indeed, it matters more, but once the basic financial needs have been realised then your team members will begin to seek fulfillment along these three axes.

Your constant challenge as a leader is that the extremes of each axis are continually pulling each of your team members in different directions.

The Self Contradictory Six Human Drives

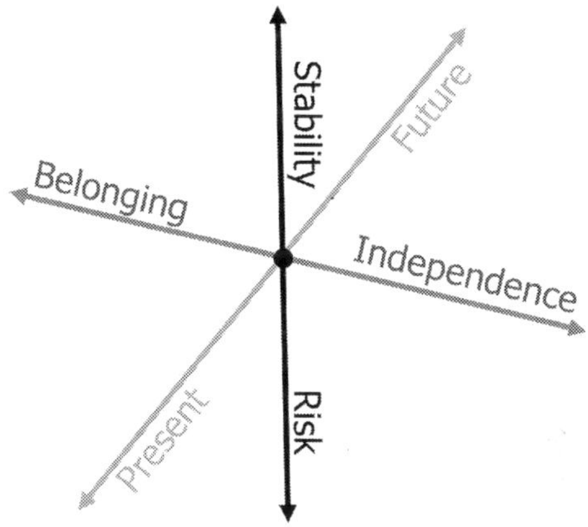

- **Autonomy:** The tension between needing to **belong** and needing to be **independent**
- **Mastery:** The tension between needing **stability** and needing to take **risks**
- **Purpose:** The tensions between **present** needs and **future** needs

At any point in time, each of your team members is living somewhere on each of these three dimensions. Yet the very act of contentment in their current position can lead to a sudden movement along one — or more — axes.

The person who lunches alone complains about cuts to the team culture budget. The team member who eschewed promotion resigns to seek new challenges. The career-driven individual who takes a sabbatical to find themselves. No sooner do you understand someone then they change.

The masculine leader grows frustrated with that

uncertainty and ambiguity. They've been trained to have the right people in the right seats on the bus, motivated by the distant destination that the bus is driving towards. How do you provide that confidence and vision, while also nurturing the ever-present complexity?

The Six Systems

Developing your personal leadership capability is important, yet in my experience systems achieve greater results because they can be implemented and managed by everyone.

Each of these six systems has been implemented in real world businesses to acknowledge the feminine energy that exists in each team member, without disempowering anyone with a masculine predisposition. As a result, they continually meet all six human drives.

1. Behaviours and Rituals (BELONGING)

Your workplace culture is the experience every team member has when they come to work today. Today, not in the future.

Yet the masculine prioritises big picture vision and mission statements. Core values that are aspirational. They lack the specific *How is our culture lived today?*

Our first system then is to document your behaviours and rituals — the "HOW" of your Culture. Behaviours are the actions that you encourage, and the ones you will not tolerate. At that level of specificity, they can be managed — and self-managed.

Rituals are those behaviours that make your organisation different, even unique. Team members who love your rituals know they won't find that experience anywhere else.

2. Personal Motivators (INDEPENDENCE)

Never lose sight of the individuality in your organisation, and the power this creates when you nurture it. As a visionary leader, do you know (and have you recorded?) the personal motivators/interests/incentives for all your team members?

In a larger enterprise, have you taught and empowered the team leaders you work with to do this also? "Discretionary effort" is a common management phrase, and it's achieved when team members feel that their individual effort can make a difference to an organisation that cares for them.

Plus you will be amazed how a few thoughtful words or a personalised gift can acknowledge and energise the individual far more than an enormous cash bonus.

3. Clear Responsibilities (STABILITY)

Nobody benefits from chaotic or ad hoc leadership. We perform when our responsibilities are clear, and we have the opportunity to execute our expertise within those clear parameters.

You can support this need through simple position descriptions, visual workflows, responsibility charts, and documented processes – all created and maintained from a nurturing space of helping your team to perform.

These are not accountability documents used to assign blame. In a culture of full responsibility, they empower your team to perform their role in relationship with everyone else's.

4. Training Program (RISK)

Risk is the most undervalued characteristic of business success, and it applies to every team member. For most, *taking a risk* means being vulnerable enough to learn and apply something new – it's a human desire to try something different and improve ourselves, while the fear of change is also common.

Does your business have a training program, with a personalised element for every team member based on their individual input? Have you trained your managers, and yourself, to encourage growth and support mistakes?

Businesses grow by taking risks. Individuals grow by taking risks.

Visionary leaders encourage those risks while also ensuring a safety net is in place.

5. Individual Contributions (PRESENT)

Maintaining a long-term vision may be integral to your business planning approach, especially as you motivate the masculine energy in your organisation. The missed opportunity in most plans is a failure to connect that future with the present.

The feminine energy in all of us is attuned to the present reality, not a distant promise. You need to ensure that each individual's contributions today are clearly connected to the larger purpose, and their actions are also acknowledged.

Have you spoken with each team member about how their role contributes to the higher outcome of the organisation? Both commercially and culturally, you will achieve long-term aspirations sooner when you and your team are connecting that future with their present.

6. Career Plans (FUTURE)

Having discussed the future of your enterprise, the final system now challenges you to value the future of your team members. Do you know the career path each of your team are seeking? Are you actively working to help them achieve their goals... even when those goals will see them leave you?

Some people will have clear aspirations, while others are more ambiguous or uncertain. As you have seen, however, these can rapidly change.

When you support your team for their future, they support you in the present. And I've seen plenty of team members whose future plans have changed when they realise how supportive their current workplace truly is, and how energised they are to remain.

Be The Change

The feminine energy values belonging, and is compassionate to individuality; it is connected to each stable moment and from that strength will nurture risk and the desire to grow; it holds space for you in the present, the better to be open for love and intimacy in the ambiguous future.

When an enterprise embraces this, each individual benefits and the organisation develops.

When leaders, supported or not, predominantly masculine or not, consciously choose to embrace the feminine they will attract the talent who value the abundant and inclusive opportunity.

References

1. Workplace Gender Equality Agency, "Gender workplace statistics at a glance", August 2018 https://www.wgea.gov.au/sites/default/files/documents/Stats_at_a_Glance.pdf

2. Guidant Financial, "Women in Business", 2021 https://www.guidantfinancial.com/small-business-trends/women-in-business

3. Australian Bureau of Statistics, "A Profile of Australian Women in Business", August 2015 https://www.pmc.gov.au/sites/default/files/publications/profile_of_australian_women_in_business.pdf

4. Dan Pink, Drive: The Surprising Truth About What Motivates Us, "RSA Animate Talk", April 1, 2010 https://www.youtube.com/watch?v=u6XAPnuFjJc https://www.danpink.com/books/drive

About Jacob Aldridge

As an international business advisor and keynote speaker, Jacob delivers results for active growth companies in Australia, Asia-Pacific, Europe, and North America.

Deeply intelligent with a keen eye for practical opportunities, Jacob's insight invites you to consider how business can be done if you avoid outdated assumptions, embrace progress, and create new paradigms on your pathway to success.

His work on *Embracing the Feminine* developed from the realisation that *Best Practice* is often anything but, and that thriving companies need visionary leaders who can leverage the fundamental differences in the masculine AND feminine approach to business.

Whether as a powerful keynote or through a targeted corporate training program, Jacob has the uncanny knack of distilling complex concepts into simple soundbites and powerful strategies that founders, executives, and team members both love… and execute.

Contact Jacob Aldridge

jacob@jacobaldridge.com

www.JacobAldridge.com

www.linkedin.com/in/jacobaldridge

Intuitive Leadership: Using 'Feminine' Intuition With Purpose

Curtis Harren

I promise that if you take the time to learn about your team's emotional needs and to intuitively lead, you will become a more effective leader.

The gender dynamics tensions that play out between different types of men and women has long been the brunt of many jokes, tales of woe, stories of heartbreak, and endless discussion about communication differences. It's true that men and women communicate differently. But that doesn't need to be a problem. Awareness of core behavior ensures we co-create the best results while allowing each to be themselves.

In fact, differences of any kind do not need to be a problem. In nature, diversity is a strength. The healthiest populations show the highest degree of diversity; genetic, biological adaptation, cultural and fit. Only humans try to manipulate this natural order. The essence of this article revolves around the word *acceptance*;

accepting others as they are, who they are, how they are. Without unhealthy criticizing judgement just for being different.

On a side note, a spiritual healer I know recently shared with me her thoughts on judgement. In short, she told me that God gave us the gift of judgment. The ability to judge whether a situation, a person, or something we are about to say or do is the safest choice. However, it is when we impart our own personal judgments on others, or impart our own beliefs, or will, to override their own; that judgement feels critical. When we feel judged, we do not feel accepted.

Conversely, to help someone feel accepted and appreciated, as a true leader it behooves us to not judge others. If you have ever recognized the frustration of someone doing something a different way than you, what did you do? Did you speak up and talk to them? Did you tell them the "better way"? If so, that likely led to them feeling judged for being different. Stop. Think about this. Have you ever felt criticized by someone you respected because you "did it a different way"? Did either person walk away feeling good? Not likely; one would likely have parted frustrated, and the other feeling attacked or unsupported.

However, when we can learn to be curious about why they chose what they chose, both parties can walk away for the better. One will feel heard and understood and the other will see a different way. This is beautiful and delivers 'real' synergy between different types of men and women.

Masculine And Feminine

We all know the differences between boy and girl, man, and woman. When my youngest first announced his true gender didn't match his body, I had to go through many transitions of my understanding of life. I always knew it to be "if I look down my pants and see dangly bits; I was a boy". Living through my child, I have come to see judgment from a very different light.

Regardless of your perspectives, or opinion on gender preferences would you accept the lines are more blurred in the context of LGTBQ? However, what if I suggested to you that gender is not only a reference to identity in sexual preferences? What if I told you the most meaningful and powerful strengths in diversity have nothing to do with gender or sexuality, it's to do with respecting differences and tuning into the person in front of you?

Stop for a moment and reflect; many languages have masculine and feminine elements. The classic romance languages like French, Spanish, even eastern European languages, including Russian. Especially if we speak any of these languages natively?

It just seems natural. Yin and yang have been used to describe the balancing of strong and soft, complementary elements of our planet as well as human life.

The foundations of the English language are, well, very diverse. Over millennia the language has adopted and adapted words from most other languages. So, while the English language doesn't employ masculine and feminine, we intuitively understand mostly what is and what isn't.

So, what does masculine and feminine really mean to you?

Well, is it simply an assignment of characteristics that are often associated with behaviors typical of men and women as experienced over centuries? Some traits may be stereotypical and others natural to each variation of human physiology.

It is important to note we all have both *types* of characteristics within us. While readily available elsewhere, it's worth spending a little time on, here are some *typical* traits of each

Masculine Traits	**Feminine Traits**
Focus on own needs	Compassionate care for others
Competitive	Collaborative
Assertive	Receptive. Grateful.
Goal Directed	Relationship Directed
Rational. Logical. Linear Thinking	INTUITIVE
Independence	Interdependence
Single Task	Multitask
Action Driven	Patience. Forgiveness
Spatial	Temporal
Left Brain	Right Brain
Logical	Creative
Strong	Soft
Forceful	Nurturing
Aggressive	Loving
Warrior	Peaceful
Assertive	Passive
Mind-Centered	Heart-Centered

Analytical	Intuitive
Emotionally Guarded	Emotional
Planning	Free Flowing
Outer	Inner
Firm	Gentle
Rational	Healing
Loyal	Wise
Adventurous	Patient
Strength	Flexible
Reason	Consideration

A lot of men recoil at the notion that they might have feminine energy...that they *might be feminine* does not mean they are female! The connotation is mis-understood due to social stereotypes However, let's explore the underlying energy behind that desire of men to discount the fact that they might have *feminine qualities. This isn't a feminine problem. It is a masculine problem.* Women have no problem accepting their masculine energy.

Why can't men accept their feminine?

Let's explore...

"Masculinity stands for a society in which social gender roles are clearly distinct: Men are supposed to be assertive, tough, and focused on material success; women are supposed to be more modest, tender, and concerned with the quality of life."

"Femininity stands for a society in which social gender roles overlap: Both men and women are supposed to be modest, tender, and concerned with the quality of life."

I hope you can see that neither is better than the other. What is better is having a balance. This doesn't mean we, as individuals, need to exhibit all, or both sides. Rather, as leaders, we need to build our teams in a way that nurtures and fosters a healthy balance while also logically and analytically driving for results. This, however, requires adopting acceptance of others, being compassionate to those involved. On the other hand, it is imperative to continue action (especially aligned and inspired) and stay the course.

Whatever your course is: business, sales, delivery, changing management styles... etc...

Logic Vs. Intuition

Logic is inherently the path of choice by most leaders. We have all heard the phrase *This is the logical thing to do*, it is something we hear all too often. However, logic has limitations. Intuition, on the other hand, is limitless and infinite. Logic creates focus and direction. Intuition offers boundless possibilities. We never know where our intuition may guide us. Yet, when we follow our intuition, this quality gives us direction.

"It is by logic that we prove, but by intuition that we discover. To know how to criticise is good, to know how to create is better."
Henri Poincare

Logic is a way of using a set of concrete rules or formulas you have learnt that you use to come up with a decision. Intuition on the other hand is a way of using abstract information you have received

LOGIC VS INTUITION

from different aspects of your life to create a sensible reasoning to come up with a decision.

I don't know about you, but as a man, I've encountered my fair share of trouble communicating with women. I've heard things like *Don't use your logic with me!, Stop being so logical!*, and many other phrases that highlight the differences between the masculine-minded and feminine-minded thinking.

For the sake of being concise, people that communicate with each other have a relationship. It might be new, such as at a first meeting, it might be a friendship, it might be something more intimate, or it might be a workplace relationship that is focused on being part of a team. So, if there are inherent communication traps such as a logical conversation during an emotional situation, you may experience a natural disparity, never mind other nuances.

Intuition is often classed as a feminine characteristic. We can argue otherwise, but let's go with that.

What is truly meant by this is that women tend to lead by their heart. They just seem to know what to do in matters of the heart, such as communication. Using this reasoning, just means that when men use their own intuition or gut instincts, they are tapping into their own heart-space. Put in more common terms, this is the old head and heart debate.

I don't know about you, but I believe business has room for both. In fact, I believe there's not enough of the heart factored into bigger business. Most businesses rely on systems and procedures to ensure efficiency and productivity. This feels rather robotic when the human element is not factored in. And since every business is composed of people, how can there not be human needs and elements of the heart? Stuff where the so-called *soft skills* are needed.

Power Of Intuition

We have all heard about women's intuition. Have you ever thought about what that really means? Is it truly just the domain of women? The answer is no. A resounding, and most definite, no! It is, however, often seen as a characteristic of feminine energy.

Many millions of dollars have been made on instinct, or intuition, alone. There are hundreds of leadership and business books on the shelf that the authors share that it was a gut feeling that's guided them. The fancy word for this is intuition. I once worked with a billionaire who was a high school dropout but who learned to trust his gut for an opportunity. I'm not kidding you when I say, he could literally smell hundreds of millions of dollars ten years into the future. I witnessed him do it.

No fancy forecasting models, no hard-hitting market research. No extravagant business plans: instead trusting in the moment when intuition lights up. (The business plan always followed though).

This does highlight the difference between men and women. A man's intuition – or gut instinct – is to be more focused around opportunity to deliver results. Whereas, a woman's intuition tends to be more around creating connections, building relationships, and fostering support, all of which will also lead to significant results in a healthy team environment. This leads me to our conversation to understanding the gender dynamics and the intelligence we can use to create the best conversations and relationships.

Gender Dynamics© Intelligence Within A Team

At risk of opening a can of worms around the topic of diversity and inclusion, are you starting to see the value, and not just the challenges of different ways of thinking and communicating? Also, I am hoping you are starting to see that gender isn't just a man versus woman scenario. For example, there are women with a high degree of orientation towards results and action, and there are also men who have a high degree of nurturing and supportive characteristics.

In exploring how differences can impact results when applied to life at work, I have had the privilege of working with Dr Pauline Crawford and her unique Gender Dynamics© Intelligence mapping instrument. This well-researched behavioral assessment is embedded in a 360 degree navigation map in which all of us exist as men and women of many types.

Using archetypes to aid real synergy between men and women, Dr Pauline proposes that there are four archetypes: masculine minded male, the RULER, feminine minded female, the SOVEREIGN, masculine minded female, The MAGICIAN and feminine minded male, the PHILOSOPHER.

There at last was me – the thinking/feeling/intuitive male leader. I came into my own power of balance within my maleness, with my intuitive feminine-minded energy

Let's be clear, these archetypes do not define our sexual orientation. They only indicate our natural reactive and potential proactive behavioural styles. For example, a masculine-minded female, Magician, is often found on executive boards, leadership roles and often will feel like she more easily fits in with men than with women. Not universally, but as an example of what this concept infers.

Likewise, a feminine-minded male, the Philosopher, is the man you may know who is caring, can navigate complex communication and seems to have an exceedingly kind heart. Both archetypes struggle with the other types of their same gender and often don't feel like they fit in.

Dr. Pauline's work and research has shown that most organizations reward and promote the masculine minded male and that the masculine minded female can succeed more easily if she chooses. However today, all the archetypes are found in the workplace and, with greater awareness, can learn to apply mutually inclusive narratives that reflect the natural differences of each style.

The goal is that using this mapping approach, as an intuitive leader, the Philosopher can raise the value of intuition, and all participate stronger together. Business working practices will then open their hearts to a more balanced culture of men and women working together.

(Note: I use the pronouns he/him and she/her intentionally. I have no disrespect intended for those who prefer they / them, the intentions of this chapter are hard to bring people together true acceptance and appreciation of difference.)

Results Of Intuitive Leadership

The answer is simple... a more cohesive team. More balance. Happier and more productive team members. Increase in creative problem solving and innovation. But, since you are reading this book, you already know this.

Connect with me. I'd love to hear from you. What results did you achieve from your intuitive leadership approach?

About Curtis Harren

After nearly 20 years in numerous employee, leadership and coaching roles; leading and being lead he has discovered the art and science of what works, what doesn't and why not. Such as taking action with respect. Having Intuitive dialogue and being accepting of others that create effective communication resulting in profitable operations.

Curtis is the proud father of two teenagers and is happily living his life fully. He loves nature and spending time in it; hiking, kayaking and even just appreciating silent moments. Curtis is also a passionate vintage motorcycle rider and amateur nature photographer. His greatest passion is seeking understanding between people.

Curtis believes that Business IS Personal. His greatest business purpose is to help transform corporations into a place their people want to work, want to do their best, and want to truly contribute.

Contact Curtis Harren, CEOcopilot

curtis@CEOcopilot.com

www.CEOcopilot.com

https://www.facebook.com/curtis.harren

https://www.linkedin.com/in/curtisharren

Tough Love

Jaime Galviz

I grew up in a family opposite to what was then considered as *traditional* for 1973 Colombia. My father and mother were from different religions but both executives running their own company.

Mom and Dad worked together complementing each other and distributing responsibilities based on what each did best, without any stereotyping about what a dad or a Mom *should* do.

Looking back, my Mom was a professional and successful woman, ahead of her time. She was the eldest daughter of a large family. From a young age, she helped raise her 13 siblings and later she managed my grandparents' finances. Not surprisingly, she handled most of the financial decisions in my family as well.

Mom was the one who created the rules, held the boundaries, assigned chores and pocket money, and determined what we could and couldn't do.

At a very young age, Dad and his siblings were abandoned by their parents. They grew up with their grandmother in very humble conditions. The school principal let them work during the recesses to help pay for their education.

Dad is softer and often, without Mom knowing, he would give us a few extra *pesos* pocket money. He also showed us his infinite love, every opportunity he had. I think Dad wanted us to feel all the parental love that he did not receive in his childhood.

My Mom ensured that while we never lacked for anything, she insisted that we grow up to be self-responsible. For example, from an early age, we worked at my parents clothing factory, even during school holidays. For me, that was *normal.*

As a ten-year-old, I could afford the things I wanted to buy, and I worked hard.

When I reached my teenage years, I noticed that most of my friends had the *same* luxuries… but they didn't have to work like I did. They were carefree and had fun.

When I went to University in Bogota, my budget was very tight. I was only able to go to the movies once a month. I worked semester breaks and full-time during vacations — I had to work so I could have some money to simply hang out — but only on weekends because Mom did not let me go out during the week!

Again, most of my classmates weren't working *and* were going out regularly, anytime.

I quickly concluded, *This isn't fair!* And I began to see my mother through different and somewhat resentful eyes. So, I decided to become independent as soon as possible.

I accelerated my university graduation by taking additional subjects in my semesters; and remained on campus, taking extra courses during vacation times.

My older sister, who worked in the technology industry, found me an internship. I confess, I would never have thought of working in IT if it wasn't for her. Funny… because I have been in IT ever since.

I was conscious of a dilemma. On one hand, my Mom was loving and affectionate and was there whenever I needed her… but at the same time, she seemed very tough. She demanded that I be responsible. I still remember her making me account for every single peso that I spent. And I resented that side of her.

For several years, I stayed away from my Mom. After graduating, I was living and working abroad, anyway, but our relationship was also distant. I wanted to avoid potential friction.

It took me several years – working, saving, buying my first apartment, getting married and becoming a father – to slowly realize that much of my drive to succeed, my work ethic, my responsibility and desire to earn, provide well and live well, were instilled in me by my mother's tough love, from an early age.

As is often the case, once I made my best life decisions; get married with the right person and having children of my own, I began to understand the positive reasons for Mom's approach. I regretted not having asked her, *Why were you like that with me?*

My wife helped me to know myself, discover my passions and despite a lot of mistakes, decide on a life plan that would honor who I *truly* wanted to be.

We agreed to raise our children in a non-American culture. Our vision was for them to grow up with a universal, more diverse, and inclusive mentality. I began to look for work where Latinos rarely work: in Asia; and in non-Spanish-speaking Europe.

As I advanced in my career, a colleague, who was looking for a COO, asked for my advice on what to expect from someone highly effective in that role. He asked me what I wanted for my next career move and I explained we were looking for a unique family lifestyle experience.

I was stunned when he asked me if I would like to go to Dubai to take on that role!

My first thought, (with all the typical biases of those who do not know that beautiful region), *I would never take my super-Catholic wife and family to a Muslim country!*

I told my colleague that this had to be a *family* decision.

We called a few friends and relatives to understand the type of lifestyle in Dubai. To our surprise, the feedback was all favorable and it seemed a perfect fit for what we wanted for our kids. We even traveled to Dubai and after two days exploring the city and its culture, we agreed.

Dubai is a safe, modern, growing city offering a great quality of life in an amazing environment. You do not feel like a foreigner: 91% of the population are not local, in a population of two million people, there were 204 nationalities.

I joined an incredibly diverse team with an

extraordinary, humble, open, vulnerable leader. At that time, we were testing and creating new ways to growth and impact the Gulf region (Qatar, Kuwait, Bahrain, Oman and UAE).

then joined the leadership team of Middle East and Africa (>80 countries, five time zones, multiple languages: some of the most vulnerable and richest countries in the world). I lead an extraordinary team and witness firsthand how technology can provide opportunities and radically change the lives of even the neediest by also co-leading our Company's Africa Strategy.

We operated in a constant VUCA environment, driven by conflicts, terrorism, political fights, natural disasters, and incredible transformational and visionary projects.

I quickly discovered empathy was our biggest ally.

Empathy supports and energizes every person, regardless of religion, politics, orientation, culture, history, and beliefs. Empathy helped us find what is common amongst different people when so *many* biases strive to keep us apart.

Our policy was: the person always comes first before the work - a challenge given the diversity of ethnicity and cultures, different holidays, days of work and personal styles of working in our team.

I now reported to a new, highly experienced female manager, who knew the region and had the right skills to move the team forward with our impact and growth objectives.

It was a steep learning curve, we had Jewish workers reporting to Palestinian managers, Turkish talent running operations with strong and very disciplined Egyptian professionals, incredible creativity from Kenyan and Nigerians, the entrepreneurship and business spirit of the Lebanese, and the unforgettable resilience and joy of South Africans.

But my greatest learnings came from working with my new boss.

She encouraged me to grow at the executive level by taking more risks and becoming bolder in the way I approached my peers and leaders.

A new person joined the team who was bold, challenging and *disruptive*. He liked to drive things his own way. In my opinion, he didn't take time to foster his peers in the right way. While we aligned on direction and disruption, we clashed on style and purpose issues and that conflict was generating a lot of unnecessary inefficiencies.

My new boss asked me to resolve the differences, without success.

She felt that despite driving impact across the region, I had untapped potential as a leader; that I was constraining myself; and I wasn't embracing friction, but in fact, I was avoiding it.

Thinking back, I knew this was my pattern of operating however I was frustrated because I couldn't see what she saw; or expected from me. That led to average on my performance reviews, which I wasn't used to.But she also did something very meaningful.

Firstly, she invested time - *several hours that was definitely not common practice,* reflecting; critiquing my strengths, impact and performance over the year and provided a very deep and direct insight into my leadership.

Her feedback felt tough.

She made it clear that I was capable of *much* better as a leader. She expected more. Specifically, I needed to be bolder and embrace friction. Her feedback challenged me in a way that felt harsh, proactive and confronting.

It reminded me of my mother's *tough love*. It felt like a sharp knife plunging into my heart, touching me to my core.

My approach was to win cooperation from my team by being soft, polite... by using humor and empathy. I knew I avoided friction and instead, tried to build cooperation and consensus because I believed it was important to get along. I avoided difficult conversations, preferring to let those moments pass, to stay silent and keep to myself. The result of this was I missed key opportunities as a leader because I didn't want to hurt others. And I wanted to be liked.

Navigating around conflicts certainly made me the nice *go-to* person, but my boss made me realize that this approach was limiting me - and my team. This had to change.

She explained why she was being tough and offered to support me through my leadership development. She role-modeled her leadership style with me, specifically, how she embraced constructive friction to better navigate uncomfortable situations.

And soon enough, I encountered opportunities with my new peer and others where I consciously generated constructive friction by sharing my points of views.

I must confess, at first I felt bad, strange, and uncomfortable. While there was tension, I gained greater clarity with my peers about what lines we were not willing to cross, how best to work with each other, and what professional agreements we would honor. We found open spaces for us to collaborate and support each other whilst leveraging our individual strengths.

As I improved, the team performed better with greater respect and consideration for each other's skills and abilities. When the pandemic hit, my team delivered a strategy to support our customers, regions, and governments in three days, despite differing points of views and frictions.

Later, my manager said she was proud that I had embraced her feedback and the leadership challenge. She noted that I was a stronger, bolder and more empathetic leader, gaining the best from myself, my team and from others.

I knew her tough love approach made that magic happen.

As leaders, peers, and friends, it is always easier to avoid those conversations, to let those moments pass by, to stay silent and keep to ourselves. We miss many opportunities to provide those gifts to others because we believe it will hurt less. But really that is cowardice, we choose not to be the one to provide the tough love because we want to be liked.

Tough love is confronting however, what makes it work is explaining *why* tough love is needed.

As a visionary leader, we must appropriately

challenge when needed, and risk making someone uncomfortable, even if it generates friction.

Wonderfully, my journey has led me to appreciate that my mother helped me grow through her tough love by giving constructive advice to help me be better. She laid the strong foundations that shaped me as a father, husband, and the leader that I am today.

Thank you, my beautiful Mom. I am truly grateful.

Tough love, done well, is invaluable.

About Jaime Galviz

Jaime Galviz has had over 20 years in leadership, innovation and delivering change collaboratively. He is passionate about helping professionals live a conscious life pursuing their own happiness. He believes in technology and education as enablers of everybody's potential and has witnessed it through his many roles in IT and innovation across more than 90 countries. He is well known for developing virtual learning platforms for millions of users. Jaime has lead initiatives in the most needed countries in Africa, Latin-America and the Middle East underpinned by respect, empathy, diversity and inclusivity to deliver meaningful results.

Contact Jaime Galviz

linkedin.com/in/jaime-galviz

twitter.com/jgalviz

Visionary Leadership At A Crucial Time in History

Dan Isaak

I have always lived by a mantra that my grandfather taught me: *"A man who never made mistakes, never made anything."*

I have learned that my mistakes have shaped me into the person I am today; and I have learned to be grateful for those opportunities for growth.

Visionary leadership has always been about embracing the unknown, no matter how vulnerable and uncomfortable navigating the unknown can be. The essence of a true visionary leader has always been the ability to visualise what others have often failed to or refused to see that shapes the goal to ultimately inspire others to positively impact the world.

I have made no secret of my opinion that business is war. Economics is no longer limited to debates about gross domestic production. Especially, when we are tested, as leadership has been tested globally, by the recent pandemic.

The pandemic has had a significant impact on the banking industry which has placed much stress on bank rates, fees and charges. The pandemic's disruption on global supply chains and financial markets has created significant pressure that has forced interest rate cuts. The ironic part of all of this is that while companys' and individuals' demand for access capital funding has skyrocketed, banks and financial services providers have in fact increased the difficulty on credit management loan qualifiers. This in simple terms means that thousands of businesses have been forced to close their doors due to a pause in trade revenue, and the banks have been unwilling to entertain any such request to offer flexible funding.

Post pandemic demands a markedly more effective corporate and government response to mitigate the aftermath of much suffering cast upon a nation's innocent civilians.

This has given me much pause for reflection about leadership. The world needs to implement productive change for the betterment of mankind who require visionary leadership skills such as an ability to:

- Focus and identify effective mission statements.
- Solidify their visions among team members.
- Commence sustainable projects with clear directives.
- Drive plans for staff provision.
- Continuously strive for improvement.
- Seek feedback from employees on improvement.

All done so with confidence, assertiveness, and respect... not arrogance. Specifically, a visionary leader mindset underpinned by emotional intelligence.

We are required to reinvent how we envisage the future, be it as an employer, a corporate leader, a government official, or a family member. If we are to be leaders who evolve and inspire, who co-create the new, we must on-board the values and beliefs that make the seemingly impossible, possible. To create emotionally responsible and sustainable work environments where talent feels empowered and supported to attempt the impossible — that is our mission for right now.

That is a delicate balancing act impacting leaders. Especially male leaders.

During my 22+ years in the banking and finance marketplace I have seen the results of an out-of-balance, toxic-masculine environment: mental illness, divorce, suicide to name a few. I have seen the loss of good people who were, and still are, simply unable to 'hang in there'.

Moving forward, I'm asking you to consider visionary male leadership; and what good looks like.

The Class Of The Modern Visionary Leader

Our pandemic world is currently in a state of chaos by degree. Whilst it isn't the first pandemic the world has experienced, it's certainly been one of the most profound and emotionally challenging disasters the world has experienced, since World War II.

This is the first-time governments have collectively governed — without a blueprint — to deploy measures globally to protect mankind.

We understand the economic and financial impact; world governments are striving to contain and resolve monetary concerns to avoid a global economic downturn. Now, we must address the emotional and social trauma. It is vital we formally acknowledge the impact to our human capital, such as mental illness and emotional fatigue.

Too often the core focus of management and leadership teams is on cutting costs via staff retrenchments. In many instances, shedding staff can prove counterproductive on an economic and social realignment process. What is already complicating this recovery is a short fall of available staffing across the board. Work-from-home initiatives provided a temporary solution for workflows, but now we are dealing with the deeper effects of trauma on existing workforces who were displaced by the pandemic; and an existential crisis of how people want to work.

This places unique practical and emotional demands on current and future leaders.

Can visionary leadership fail?

In principle, *yes*. Consider this.

Visionary leadership often identifies the need for strategic change, but usually, change is what we are scared of most.

Leaders have ideas that disrupt, that cause friction; that can clash and collide when mid-level management is not in bipartisan agreement. Dialogues stall. If you are in a senior leadership role you have already experienced this to some degree — even on benign issues. You've experienced distinctions between ranks let alone two people who don't think the same. You've experienced silos and factions within the same organisation. And leaders whose decision-making is arbitrary in nature, resulting in a leader being misaligned with the executive board's directives.

In my own experience within the banking sector, the longer the group of senior management displayed resistance, the more separation occurred, eventually causing a rift between the board and the remaining executive directors.

But I am hopeful that world-class visionary leadership is possible. And I am reflecting on the qualities of a successful, progressive high-level visionary male leader.

Here's my current best thinking:

1. Effective Communicators

Visionary leaders are extremely effective at sharing their dream and ideas with others who identify and include shared values between their vision for the business; and the personal values of their team. Often they use their qualification and experience to express sensible and balanced future objectives to the numbers, especially when it's in the best interests of those involved.

2. Strategic Planners

They give sensible consideration as to the preparation required to select and implement the best vision and strategic methodologies moving forward within a more equitable and sustained context.

3. Risk Aware

With any risk, even the balanced ones, there is never a certainty that can be factored or calculated to guarantee that a strategy pans out perfectly. Leaders must have a genuine ability to reduce and mitigate any risks posed. They must reduce any potential impact to the lives of others balancing contingent liabilities of failure outweighed by the probability of success.

4. Influential As Change Managers

They have the ability to be emotionally convincing in matters of transformation. The emphasis is on the development of the team, as a whole. They demonstrate competent stewardship and performance in how they play out their own department roles. Or by putting departments and functions in place that will aid the everyday operation of the organisation.

5. Mutual Support Innovation

They must have the ability to project beyond their own ability to see the future. Emotional intelligence gives these leaders the ability to recognise that in many instances the best way to make progress is to trust their own team to take risks of their own, instead of always being stuck in the status quo when ushering new projects, acquisitions, or initiatives.

Confident visionary leaders are comfortable with their decision to trust and accept their team's realistic potential of failure is real, which can impact the entire project. They understand that progress is made, by learning from errors — whether human, or process.

6. Be Extremely Tenacious

Ironically, visionary leaders have usually experienced periods of turbulence within their respective areas of expertise and tend to have a high level of emotional and mental resilience. They have cultivated their capacity to overcome and bounce back in times of disruption, without engaging in dysfunctional behaviour. They can draw on their prior experience — good and bad — to adapt to the current situation when they are up against the odds, no matter what it is.

7. Capacity And Maturity To Hold The Vision

Often, they're so intense, their purpose can be mistaken for insanity, when in fact it's purely a position of visionary maturity they hold beyond the current understanding of others. They generally do not let the opinions of others sway their purpose because often have the experience to assess the long-reaching effects of ill-conceived opinions. Only with results do *Thomas the Doubters* then become believers in the vision. It is with this self-control, centred in a healthy, balanced self-belief, that they inspire others.

Importantly they demonstrate integrity. It is to follow a leader that does not exhibit the traits being requested. As Ghandi said; ... *be the change you want to see in the world.*

8. Eccentrically Proud

Visionary leaders have the ability to see — or unearth — what no one else can, be it in finding new opportunities, innovations, products, pivots... even life saving ideas.

Superglue, was first developed by scientists at Eastman Kodak during WWII to repair gun sights for military use. Although it was a visionary leader who discovered that super glue could be used on combat soldiers to stem the bleeding from severe injuries sustained during battle. As a result, hundreds if not thousands of lives were saved. Only years later did it become a household product for domestic use.

I have speculated on what good looks like. But there's a flip side.

The following is a snapshot of issues I have experienced at leadership level operating in a heavily regulated industry that is desperate for visionary leadership. Let's call them mistakes:

Tunnel-Vision

I have seen it all too many times when a leader becomes infatuated with outcomes so much so that they stop paying attention to the finer details. Worse, when they lose sight of their original vision and rationale. Become aware of what tunnel vision looks and feels like, for you.

Lost Sight/Focus

Leaders who become distracted to the point that they lose sight of what they initially intended to address within the specified time. Knowing, and connecting, to *why* is paramount to staying focused on holding your vision.

Weak Minded Under Pressure

The ability to carry on and become your strongest in the absence of key people due to unforeseen circumstances will become the driving force of the project being carried out successfully. I've seen leaders crumble under benign pressures. Keep strength of mind to carry on. Explore times where you have demonstrated resilience… and times where you cave in. Reflect. Dig deeper.

And if you need help — ask for it.

No Faith

Visionary leaders must develop the ability to cultivate other individuals who may be losing belief during the project. Only through emotional intelligence and sincere leadership can one continue to keep the support from all members. Without all troops staying committed to the dream, the project can be put in jeopardy of completion. It is embarrassing, avoidable and costly when a leader succumbs to a lack of faith. Keep the faith in the bigger picture, especially when no one else does.

Shifting, Poor Or Unclear Priorities Kill The Dream

Leaders per se usually need to reinvent, adjust, realign. When a leader becomes set in their ways it can jeopardise the entire objective. When in doubt, order your priorities. Remember why you started, course correct and stay on target. If it means altering future planning, do it. Be open to learning. If you don't respect this simple rule, it could result in the team at large losing total faith, worse still may be the difference between success or abandonment of the entire joint venture altogether. Centre into your priorities to keep the dream alive.

Say One Thing, Do Another

The essence of true leadership is congruence. The talk and the walk align. True leadership is not about titles, positions, seniority or flow charts. It's about integrity. Wholeness. It's the ability to positively influencing others through demonstration. Lead by example.

Ducking The Challenge

We all know or know of leaders who side-stepped the challenges. Leadership is essentially about making the lives of others better, as a result of your presence and making sure that the impact you leave becomes a lasting legacy in your absence. Visionary leaders do not duck challenges. They step up. Lean in. Stay true.

It's an entry level snapshot, sure. The above mistakes are systemic of a lack of, or lapse in, emotional intelligence.

A starting point might be to reflect on the mistakes. You may then discover qualities and areas that relate specifically to your world. Identify the mistake, reflect on why it's a mistake, discover examples of those who made or corrected that mistake; and what good looks like in a meaningful visionary leadership context.

I don't know you personally or your challenges. But I am asking you to reflect on what visionary leadership looks like, to you. Its needed now.

Notice if you align visionary to something disparaging or negative. Do you believe that vulnerability is a form of weakness? That assumption is almost always profoundly dangerous and misguided.

Visionary leaders are usually challenged to embrace vulnerability in their quest to benefit others. Emotional intelligence underpins that quest.

I'd love to hear your feedback...

About Dan Isaak

Dan Isaak has been involved within the advisory, financial services and banking industry for more than 20 years providing access to commercial lending and senior venture capital for corporate entities and entrepreneurs; residential and commercially secured mortgages; and helping businesses access general funding and flexible lending alternatives to major banks.

Dan has a broad range of personal interests such as sports, recreational outdoor activities, as well as humanitarian interests in supporting poverty and is a passionate supporter for all those brave people battling cancer. Please donate www.pinkribbon.com.au or www.cancer.org.au

Coming from humble beginnings, Dan has always held an important quote close to his heart:

A rich person isn't one who has the most, it's the one who needs the least.

Contact Dan Isaak

dan@stroghurstblack.com

https://www.privatelendersaustralia.com.au/

https://www.linkedin.com/in/danisaak/

Why I Champion Conscious Empathic Leadership

Alan Wick

My title could have read *Why I Champion Conscious Empathic Leadership In Men*, to emphasise the extra importance of men having to work more consciously at displaying empathic behaviours in their leadership, but that feels just as sexist as saying that female leaders need to 'man up'!

Traditional 'male' characteristics like decisive, powerful, authoritarian and abrasive are not solely displayed by men, any more than traditional 'female-labelled' characteristics like empathy, tolerance, vulnerability, sustainability and intuition are displayed only by women. Many male and female leaders demonstrate a mix of both.

Leadership traits are not gender specific!

There's no denying the historical male/female divide however, with power and opportunity dramatically weighed towards men. Women have been suppressed for decades, subconsciously as well as consciously.

In recent years there's been a cultural shift in the Western world. The way women have systemically been treated as inferior is being challenged and overturned. Women are being treated with greater respect and their voices are increasingly being heard.

This is long overdue. However, the harsh truth is, for a lot of (especially) older men in executive leadership positions their ingrained perceptions of the male/female dynamic run deep. It takes a colossal amount of conscious effort to overturn these entrenched prejudices.

I speak from personal experience when I say that this effort is well worth it. It reaps huge rewards for leaders who can shift their own behaviours, both for themselves and for everyone around them.

My own leadership style has changed over the last 20 years. I used to demonstrate incredibly 'male' characteristics. I founded, built and sold five companies in 25 years, the epitome of a single-minded, target-driven approach to business, quite oblivious to the effect I had on other people or how I communicated with them. The impact of my words and actions just wasn't on my radar. I was tunnel-visioned and purely results-oriented.

Then, a series of bad experiences in business stopped me in my tracks. I stepped back, took stock, listened to the nagging voice inside me that was telling me something wasn't right. My successes felt hollow and my soul felt empty. As I unpicked my behaviours and examined what was truly important, I slowly evolved into the leader I am today.

I had always believed that love in business was an

interesting concept; however, it had been a small voice that was drowned out as I chased financial results.

Now, I consciously encourage that side of me to flourish. I connected my values to how I conducted my business relationships.

What does *love in business* mean to me?

Stereotypically, in the business world some leaders are embarrassed by the word love and find it an incongruous fit. They've shied away from the word itself. Yet love doesn't have to mean lovey dovey... hearts and flowers... the 'woo-woo' stuff. For me, the very definition of love in business can be distilled into two words: purpose and passion.

And the facts bear this approach out.[1]

That's why I believe in purpose-led businesses. That means doing business with care, empathy, engagement, tough love and radical candour[2] at times — though always grounded in the value of love. It means being connected to a greater good, a desire to make a positive impact for the people you work with, your customers, the planet, and the world at large. In other words, the *'Triple Bottom Line' = People, Planet and Profit.*[3]

To want to make money is a given. However, without a purpose, we are chasing short-term goals with no lasting fulfillment, either personally or professionally. To lead a business that values influence over profit, and does business in a way that balances commerce and compassion; putting long-term sustainability ahead of short-term profit, you must authentically live the leadership qualities that epitomise these values.

Through my own experience and that of so many others', I feel it's vital that business and love are intertwined. How important this is, in addition to the impact it has across your business ecosystem, can't be underestimated. Traditional male characteristics have been seen as the 'hard' side of business and traditional female characteristics have been seen as the 'soft' side of business.

Robert Haas, Chairman and CEO of Levi Strauss & Company, said, "What we've learned is that the soft stuff and the hard stuff are becoming increasingly intertwined. A company's values — what it stands for, what its people believe in — are crucial to its competitive success. Indeed, values drive the business."

You must ensure that your business has a defined, articulated Purpose and Values; think of it as *Purpose + Values = DNA* or, if you prefer, *Culture*. Then, you have a foundation on which you can build and actively manage your business's DNA. The benefits of building and managing your business's DNA include:

1. Increasing employee retention.
2. Attracting and recruiting better talent.
3. Strengthening your brand's reputation.
4. Improving productivity through a happier, more engaged team.
5. Making better decisions.
6. Boosting your P&L.
7. Increasing shareholder value.[4]

You can't manage your business's DNA in isolation. You can, however, lead by example, through your consistent, considerate, respectful and motivational behaviours. Be constantly mindful that the right people are your business's most important asset — hire slowly, fire quickly. Think about how you're going to attract and retain, lead, manage and motivate your team.

As a leader, it's your job to 'own' the environment and be in tune with the atmosphere. Is there any friction? Any resentment? Any insecurities or misconceptions? Negative situations like these need to be identified and resolved honestly and transparently.

There could be die-hard prejudices at play.

It's common, for example, to have an atmosphere of unconscious bias against women; intrinsically feeling that they're inferior — that their opinions don't carry the same weight as a man's around a boardroom table. A woman in this situation can feel unheard, out-numbered and frustrated, which can then spiral into withdrawal and self-doubt. An empathic and relationship-oriented leader will pick up on this and manage the dynamics to equalise the voices in the room.

The business world is changing fast, partly driven by Gen X, Millennials and Gen Z entering the workplace — all with very different expectations from Baby Boomers. Openness towards, discussion about, and the platform given to mental wellbeing, has exploded. With the amount of time people spend at work, it's inevitable and absolutely right that this shift in understanding, and awareness of and sensitivity towards people's mental health, is becoming more and more inextricably woven into leadership styles that are fit for purpose in today's environment — traditional feminine traits like compassion, deep-listening, patience, generosity and emotional intelligence, to name a few.

It can be hugely challenging for 'old school' male leaders to evolve their leadership style into this newer consciousness. Just like an elite golfer who changes their golf swing technique halfway through their career, it can take a mammoth effort, intense concentration and sustained hard work to make the change. However, their results show that it is worth it.

Leading with purpose — with love — expands beyond the leader's fulfillment to create a more harmonious environment, leading to a happier, more secure, more productive and thriving workforce who will generate better quality output and a more profitable business for all.[4]

A recent survey[5] of over 2,000 employees in the UK found that 55% had left their jobs because of bad management, with the majority of respondents saying they didn't think managers were equipped to deal with the human or emotional sides of their jobs. This resonated with me and really highlights the importance of this transformation in how we approach leadership.

Just saying the words *love in business* like a mantra is not much use. It needs a practical application in business. It's about engagement.

So, what is your approach to running your business? How do you engage with your colleagues, your team, your suppliers, and your clients? Do you acknowledge your colleagues, clients or suppliers when they do a good job?

And don't forget yourself!

Are you open, genuine and transparent in the way that you deal with people? What about a spirit of partnership in your approach to business? Love in business is all about relationships rather than transactions. Relationships created through shared values — how often have you been offered a big contract but you're doubtful about how your business would be treated by the client? Of course, business is not all a bowl of cherries and sometimes you have to let people go. I call it tough love. You can still be caring, though you have to challenge directly and honestly.

An interesting scenario I'm picturing, where the effectiveness of a visionary male leader approach is demonstrated, is an early-stage niche medical instruments manufacturer I know of. Sitting on a goldmine of potential, having invented a revolutionary, perfectly timed and highly sought after new product, this company is projected to be valued at £50m in five years' time. The founder has recruited 'big guns' for the board with a weight of experience and success behind them. He has also brought a female marketing expert with him from a previous company, who is ambitious and aiming to be board level in the future. However, the perception of her and treatment towards her by the all-male board has a lot of room for improvement. The atmosphere is crackling with the eager anticipation they're all feeling. You could say it's a testosterone-fuelled environment. Their eyes are on the prize; they're single-mindedly driving the business towards the jackpot that's awaiting them if all goes well. It's a tricky dynamic — making sure everyone feels secure and valued so that they can all perform at their optimum level for the combined good of the company. Achieving this requires the founder to embrace emotional intelligence and harness 'feminine' leadership traits.

Let's go back to the key word in the title of this chapter — *empathy* — and deep-dive into its meaning.

Empathy is about assuming someone else's life circumstances, walking a mile in their shoes to genuinely understand what they are going through. It starts with listening. Listening with a view to understanding sets the scene for a relationship built on trust. A good leader forms an alliance with their colleagues, stands in the trenches with them, experiences the highs and lows and is always ready to hear what their colleagues have to say. Empathy also means that understanding flows in both directions. A good leader will hear their team out and listen well, and also communicate well too; being generous in sharing their knowledge and insights.

It's telling that, when I define six qualities of good leaders, they are grounded in the so-called feminine leadership traits. They are:

1. Empathise and have self-awareness.
2. Prioritise personal and professional development.
3. Focus on developing others.
4. Encourage strategic thinking, innovation and action.
5. Espouse the values of the business and are ethical.
6. Communicate effectively.

As a leader, ask yourself how many of the six qualities can you confidently tick? This list is a fantastic benchmark for sense checking your leadership style. Do you have the attributes to be an effective leader today and all the tomorrows to come? And, if you don't, are you self-aware enough to realise it — an attribute that's often the biggest hurdle for many leaders. Then, are you willing to put the work in to evolve, grow and improve? If you are, the sense of purpose, joy and fulfillment you'll receive in return will be priceless… as well as the level of your business success.

Footnotes

1. In the book "Firms of Endearment: How World-Class Companies Profit from Passion and Purpose", the authors measured 28 corporations over a two-year period, 18 of which were publicly listed, using this model. These widely-loved public companies outperformed the S&P 500 by huge margins, over ten-, five-, and three-year time horizons. The public "FoEs" returned 1,026 percent for investors over the ten years ending June 30, 2006, compared to 122 percent for the S&P 500; that's more than an 8-to-1 ratio!

2. Scott. K (Author) (2019). Radical Candour. Pan Macmillan.

3. Elkington. J (Author) (1999). Cannibals with Forks: The Triple Bottom Line of 21st Century Business. Capstone.

4. A recent Deloitte Insights report found that purpose-driven companies witness higher market share gains and grow three times faster on average than their competitors, all while achieving higher workforce and customer satisfaction.

5. A YouGov survey of 2,006 employees, conducted in 2018 on behalf of HR and payroll solutions provider MHR.

About Alan Wick

Alan Wick is a renowned business coach and management consultant who has specialised in supporting growth-minded entrepreneurs for 20 years. Prior to this, he spent 25 years founding, growing, scaling and selling businesses nationally and internationally. This experience has been key to helping his clients take their businesses where they want them to go (one of the companies he led won two Queen's Awards for Export and one Queen's Award for Innovation). Alan guides small business owners by sharing his experiences and stories, helping them overcome their obstacles to reach their goals more quickly and with less stress, through a rigorous process underpinned with love. This leads to a future with increased profits and impact, without working longer hours. He is purpose-led, values influence over profit, and does business in a way that balances commerce and compassion, putting long-term sustainability ahead of short-term profit.

Contact Alan Wick

lovebusiness@alanwick.com

www.alanwick.com

www.facebook.com/alanwicklovebusiness

www.instagram.com/alancwick

www.linkedin.com/in/alanwick

https://twitter.com/alanwick

Would You like To Contribute To Future Editions of *Visionary Male Leaders*?

If you would like to contribute to future editions of *Visionary Male Leaders* please contact Sarah Bellorini via LinkedIn

sarah@sarahbellorini.com

Printed in Great Britain
by Amazon

68734567R00104